BRADFI____

a history of an Essex village

for Judith

from

Sue Cunningham.

Written & published by

The Friends of St Lawrence Church Bradfield

BRADFIELD – a history of an Essex village

Written & published by:

The Friends of St Lawrence Church Bradfield
www.fslbradfield.org

ISBN : 978-0-9575490-0-5

Printed by: AutoPrint, Harwich

To

"Topsy"

Acknowledgements

This book is dedicated to Doreen "Topsy" Agnew in recognition of her untiring work, enthusiasm and dedication in collecting together village stories and memories over the years for the new millennium. Topsy died in 2010 in her hundredth year and it was her aim to publish a Bradfield history. The authors have made extensive use of Topsy's files in producing this book and they are greatly indebted to her and all of the villagers who contributed their stories and recollections towards her records. It has not been possible to use all of Topsy's material in this short book, but her full files will be preserved as part of an archive of Bradfield's history.

The Friends are also most grateful to all of the many local historians whose individual research has greatly helped in the planning of this book. There are too many to mention here, but in particular both Nigel Klammer's and Shelagh Tate's vast knowledge and help have been invaluable. Denis Bayley's 1962 book "Bradfield Church Essex" has been very useful to the authors for information about the parish church and the Grimston family history.

All of the 1875 Ordnance Survey maps used in Chapter 5 of this book are reproduced by courtesy of Essex Record Office.

This is a Friends publication but has been written by a small team of members who have spent many hours researching and compiling this short history of Bradfield. The Friends committee would also, therefore, like to thank Bob Coe and the other members of the history group - Margaret Attfield, Ted Beckwith, Ron Brown, Sue Cunningham and Wendy Ellis - for their time and effort in making this book become a reality, and also Henry Lambon for his illustrations.

CONTENTS

Introduction

Bradfield is a small village on the south side of the River Stour in the north east corner of Essex, between Manningtree to the west and Harwich to the east. It is, perhaps, of little significance to the world at large but, like all other villages everywhere, it is special because it has its own individual identity and unique history. Despite much being known about Bradfield's history from individual and group research over the years, no book has been written. The Friends of St Lawrence Church, Bradfield's parish church, therefore decided to commission and write this book – "Bradfield – a history of an Essex village".

In this short history the authors have looked back as far as possible to try to give some clue as to Bradfield's earliest origins and to describe its changes and development over the centuries. It starts way back in the Stone Age, briefly covers Roman and Anglo-Saxon times before looking in some detail at the community that existed here shortly after the Norman Conquest, as provided in the fascinating Domesday records of what was by then an established feudal manor. It then traces the development of the village through medieval times looking at the interesting lives of successive family "dynasties" of the lords of the manor of Bradfield. Where appropriate it looks briefly at national events that would have affected life in rural Essex.

Whereas the early chapters of the book are a factual record of Bradfield's history, in the remainder of the book we look more closely at how life in the village has changed over the last century or so. We pause in 1881 to take a more detailed look at life in the village, by which time the impact of the industrial revolution over the previous century had made significant changes. The census of that year provides an intriguing glimpse of the people and their trades and we take a walk around the village referencing to a detailed Ordnance Survey map of that time. Next we move on to look at some of the significant events that affected village life in the 20th century before concluding with a brief glimpse of life in Bradfield in the early 21st century.

This book is not an academic history of Bradfield but a basic reference guide and it is hoped that some readers will be encouraged to carry out further research into Bradfield's history. The authors apologise for any inaccuracies or omissions in this book.

Chapter 1

Early Days

Some key historical dates:-

- c4500 - 2000 BC   New Stone Age
- c2000 – 800 BC   Bronze Age
- c800 BC – 50 AD   Iron Age/Celtic Britain
- c50 - 410 AD   Roman Britain
- c410 – 1066 AD   Anglo-Saxons

One of the difficulties in writing a history of any village is to know exactly where to start. Groups of hunter gatherers would have roamed across the land for millennia, but at what point they decided to settle and build a community is lost in the mists of time. In Bradfield's distant past someone must have thought that the fertile land and river location was good enough to want to settle down, but when exactly this was will always remain a mystery. What we do know is that the village's name has Anglo-Saxon origins and means "broad field", but it is likely that there had been a settlement of some sorts here for centuries beforehand.

Although there is little early archaeological evidence of a settlement at Bradfield, one most significant find was made in 1997. In the garden of a house in Crow Hall Lane, off Heath Road, a pre-historic axe head was unearthed which was sent to the Colchester Museum for appraisal.

It turned out that it was a Stone Age axe of rather special significance. The museum described the axe as:

"a flint axe, flaked all over the exterior surface, no evidence of polishing. Trapezoidal shape, narrow rounded butt, semi-circular blade, pointed oval section, parallel faces. Excellent (mint) condition, no signs of wear on blade or butt. Complete."

The axe measures about six and a half inches long and three inches wide. It was made sometime between 4000 and 2000 BC.

Apparently such finds in perfect condition are very rare. As a result, it has been named "The Bradfield Stone Axe" and is on display at Colchester Museum. Most Stone Age axes that are found are in used or broken condition, having been discarded after agricultural activities, such as the clearance of woodland to create

fields around settlements. However, because of the perfect condition of the Bradfield Axe, the museum has suggested two alternative explanations. One possibility is that the axe was part of a hoard or group of axes buried in the ground for safe-keeping

The "Bradfield Stone Axe" (photo: M Scurrell)

as part of the stock-in-trade of an axe-maker. Another explanation is that it was a ritual offering of some kind to the gods. We shall probably never know but it is fascinating to have this evidence of ancient civilization at Bradfield.

There are a few other archaeological finds from the Bradfield area which are worth a mention. In 1874 a "beehive puddingstone quern" (a hand grinding stone dating from the last century BC) was found in Bradfield providing evidence of agricultural activities in the area. Part of a Neolithic sickle was found near Bradfield Hall as well as a small Bronze Age axe near Whitehouse Farm.

The Romans

Emperor Claudius invaded Britain in 43 AD and Bradfield was under Roman rule from the start. Nearby Camulodunum (now Colchester) was the first Roman town to be established.

Although we have no specific evidence of a settlement at Bradfield in Roman times it does seem likely that there was something here. We know there was a Roman settlement in Mistley and also one near Harwich. According to a history of Manningtree, *"it has been suggested that there was a Roman route running to a ferry terminal on the Stour, possibly near Nether Hall, Bradfield. The ferry ran across the Stour to what is now called Graham's Wharf at Stutton, from where there is evidence of a Roman road running into the middle of Ipswich and on to the north, possibly forming an alternative route to the main Roman road that crossed the Stour at Flatford".*

A few Roman coins have come to light, in particular a "denarius" of Augustus, who was the first emperor of Rome from 31 BC to 14 AD. Fragments of Roman bricks, tiles and pottery have been found close to St Lawrence Church.

Before the Roman invasion Essex was ruled by the Trinovantes, one of the Celtic tribes of pre-Roman Britain and considered to be the most powerful in the land. Their territory was on the north side of the Thames estuary in current Essex and Suffolk and included lands now located in Greater London. They were bordered to the north by the Iceni, and to the west by the Catuvellauni. Their capital was Camulodunum. The Trinovantes were the first tribe to establish important trade links and friendship with Rome.

Initially, the Trinovantes co-operated with the Romans until loss of tribal territory caused them to join forces with the Iceni under the command of Boudicca. In 61 AD the Iceni burnt Colchester to the ground. The resulting harsh Roman revenge on both tribes meant that Essex was firmly under Roman control until they left Britain around 410 AD.

The Anglo-Saxons

We have no real knowledge of life in Bradfield in Anglo-Saxon times. After the Romans left, Britain became an easy target for foreign invasion. In East Anglia especially people were open to attack. The Saxons were quick to raid the coastal areas of Essex and then continued westwards. These raiders were looters and destroyers and moved on rather than settled. However, when the warriors moved further inland families and true settlers came behind them and by about 600 AD the Anglo-Saxons had colonised much of England. They were basically farmers who had themselves been driven off their lands in Europe.

The Saxons were known to have sailed up the river Stour as early as 442 AD and many would have settled within easy access of the river for the benefit of the fishing and ease of moving from place to place. The name Bradfield, from "broad field", suggests that the highly forested land south of the river was cleared and farming developed during Anglo-Saxon times.

3

The Christian church had been well established in Roman Britain, but it suffered greatly from the invasions. All the Anglo-Saxon kings were pagans. Gradually, however, over the centuries, missionaries would succeed in bringing Christianity back to East Anglia. The conversion to Christianity of East Anglian kingdoms began in 597 AD when Pope Gregory I sent St Augustine to Britain.

Slowly the Saxons worked towards unified rule, but they in turn were challenged by the Danes' continued raids a century or two later. The only way the Saxons could counter the Danes was to buy them off. Essex, along with other eastern counties of England, had to pay vast sums (raised by taxes – "Danegeld") to pay the Danes not to make further attacks. This worked for a while until the next raid started the whole process over again.

The church of St Lawrence is, far and away, Bradfield's oldest surviving building. Although the current building, with its many changes and restorations over the centuries, dates back to the 1200s it is thought that there was an even older building beneath the current foundations which probably dated back to Anglo-Saxon times.

Artist's impression of how Bradfield's Anglo-Saxon church may have looked. (Drawn by Henry Lambon)

Chapter 2

The Norman Conquest

Some key historical dates;-

- 1042   Edward the Confessor
- 1066   Harold II
- 1066   William / Norman invasion
- 1086   Domesday survey
- 1087   William II
- 1100   Henry I

Although we know very little about Bradfield's early history, we do get a fascinating glimpse of what life must have been like shortly after the Norman Conquest from the Domesday Book, published in 1086. This survey provides information on over 13,000 settlements in England and Wales.

After the Norman invasion in 1066 William needed to defend England from possible invasion threats from Scandinavia. He was also involved with various costly campaigns being fought in northern France. His vast army required substantial funding and that meant taxing the people. Interestingly he did this by using a uniform tax inherited from the Anglo-Saxons (Danegeld). In order to determine the wealth of the country and how it should be taxed, in 1086 he set about making a detailed study of the population. William's survey was later to be dubbed the "Domesday Survey" – the nature of the information collected led people to compare it to the Last Judgement, or "Doomsday", described in the Bible. It was a massive task and from it William had a comprehensive assessment of the potential amount of tax he could raise from his subjects and their assets. There were, in fact, two Domesday surveys. The main one covered most of the country but "Little Domesday", which came later, just covered Essex, Suffolk and Norfolk. More detailed information was obtained for Little Domesday than the rest of the country, which is fortunate as far as this book is concerned, as we can gain quite a good knowledge of Bradfield at that time.

There are three references to Bradfield in the Domesday book - the main village Bradfelda (Bradfield), a hamlet Manestuna (Bradfield Manston) and also a small holding. According to the survey, prior to the Norman Conquest, Aluric Camp was lord of the manor of Bradfield. Aluric was one of Edward the Confessor's prized champions who had been rewarded for his loyalty with many properties. Alfelm held Bradfield Manston and Leofwine the small holding.

These are the actual extracts from the Domesday book for Bradfield and Bradfield Manston:-

Bradfield Domesday entry:

Bradfield Manston Domesday entry:

The manor at Bradfield covered an area of four and a half hides and had one saltpan. Bradfield Manston was one hide and twenty-five acres in size and had one saltpan and one and a half acres of meadow. The small holding covered half a hide and fifteen acres.

A "hide" was an area of land, usually the amount held adequate to support one free family and its dependants. It was not a standard measure and varied in area from place to place depending upon the quality of the soil, but was generally between 60 and 120 acres.

We know that the manor of Bradfield Manston was close to where Jacques Hall and Ragmarsh Farm are today. It is likely that the manor at Bradfield was either nearer the church or perhaps near where Nether Hall is today. Both manors had saltpans, which implies an estuary location, and the church (which was probably there by this time) stands on a hill conveniently mid-way between the two. Bradfield Hall, almost a mile away, was not built until the 1500s, so probably only became the manorial seat well after the Domesday survey.

The survey provided information about the size of each settlement, the number of family heads living there, sub-divided into the various classes under the strict hierarchal feudal structure, together with information about their livestock. This was not just a snapshot picture as this information was determined as at three separate dates - (a) prior to the Norman Conquest, (b) immediately after and (c) in 1086, when the survey was made. The survey also served as a gauge of the country's economic and social state in the aftermath of the Conquest and the unrest that followed it.

Under the feudal system people were categorised as "freemen", "villeins", "bordars" or "serfs". A freeman was a person who was not under the control of the lord of the manor and possessed the rights and privileges of a citizen. A villein was a tenant who was tied to the lord of the manor but who had a share in the agricultural system of the manor. He was above the status of a slave, but was assumed to be annexed to the lord's person. In return for his landholding he was obliged to perform a variety of services and make payments to the lord. A bordar was allowed to cultivate some land to give him subsistence, but he was obliged to perform menial work for the lord either free or for a fixed sum. A serf (slave), the lowest feudal class, was attached to the land owned by a lord and required to perform labour in return for certain legal or customary rights.

Rather than provide a strict translation of the Domesday text it is perhaps convenient to summarise the survey information in a table. Below is the Domesday information for both Bradfelda and Manestuna:

Bradfield (Bradfelda)	(4.5 hides + one saltpan)		
	Pre-1066	Post-1066	1086
Freemen	0	0	0
Villeins	7	4	4
Bordars	10	10	10
Serfs	2	2	2
Lord's ploughs	2	2	2
Men's ploughs	7	7	3
Pigs	20	20	33
Cows	4	4	4
Sheep	100	100	100
Valuation of manor	£7	£7	£3

Note: Domesday states that "of this manor a certain wife of a knight of his holds half a hide and is worth 10 shillings (50p) in the valuation"

Bradfield Manston (Manestuna)			(One hide and 25 acres + one saltpan and a two acre meadow)

	Pre-1066	Post-1066	1086
Freemen	0	0	0
Villeins	1	1	1
Bordars	4	4	3
Serfs	1	1	1
Lord's ploughs	2	2	1
Men's ploughs	1	1	0
Pigs	15	15	15
Sheep	15	15	15
Valuation of manor	£4	£4	£1

The smallholding, of half a hide and fifteen acres, which was held by Loefwine, had one bordar, one serf and one plough, but by 1086 there were none. The land was worth 40 shillings (£2) before the Conquest, 30 shillings (£1.50) in 1066 but only five shillings (25p) by 1086.

It should be noted that the Domesday survey only counted household heads. The families of those household heads were not counted, nor were any monks or nuns living in the settlement. It is generally accepted that the total headcount of those surveyed should be multiplied by about four or five to arrive at an estimate of the population as a whole. It is likely, therefore, that the total population of the Bradfield lands was about 100 – 120.

After his victory in 1066, William immediately went about ousting all Anglo-Saxon lords from their estates, replacing them with Norman lords and other high ranking people who had supported his conquest. They were given these estates as a reward. Domesday records that Roger de Ramis was lord of both manors at Bradfield (Bradfield and Bradfield Manston) at that time. He was in fact Roger de Raimes (from northern France), Ramis being the Latinised version of the name. The smallholding held by Leofwine was granted to Roger de Poitou (sometimes referred to as Roger Pictaviensis) by William.

What seems to be apparent by looking at the above statistics is that Bradfield declined somewhat over the 20 years after the Norman invasion. Not only did the population decrease, but so did its valuation in quite a dramatic way. Strangely, perhaps, this is in sharp contrast with the village's closest neighbour, Wix, where over the same period the population grew and the manorial valuation increased from six pounds ten shillings to ten pounds. Both Roger de Ramis and Roger de Poitou were given many estates and it is probable that both rarely visited Bradfield and would have relied on others to run the manors. Neither Bradfield nor Bradfield Manston had any freemen, so possibly other Norman knights ran these properties on their behalf. Wix on the other hand had prospered under the patronage of Queen Editha, the wife of Edward the Confessor. She favoured William the Conquerer's claim to the throne rather than that of Harold and therefore after the conquest was able to keep her lands. Perhaps for these reasons Wix prospered whilst Bradfield declined.

For comparison purposes here is a brief summary of some of the key Domesday numbers for Bradfield's neighbouring villages:-

	Mistley		Wix		Wrabness	
	pre1066	1086	pre1066	1086	pre1066	1086
Freemen	0	0	0	0	0	0
Villeins	0	0	14	14	6	6
Bordars	15	15	18	28	8	8
Serfs	4	1	4	3	6	6
Value	£3	£3	£6.50	£10	£6	£6

More key historical dates;-

- 1135   Stephen
- 1154   Henry II
- 1189   Richard I
- 1199   John
- 1215   Magna Carta signed
- 1216   Henry III
- 1272   Edward I

Life at that time must have been tough but at least there was a hierarchal structure that, despite its apparent unfairness to us today, stood the test of time for centuries. Under feudalism everybody knew their place and even at the lowest levels there were both advantages and disadvantages.

Feudalism brought people together to serve a common interest. There were many dangers and uncertainties in medieval times and the feudal system helped to bring about stability and security. People joined together in response to problems such as the risk of foreign invaders, the lack of a common currency or trade and food shortages. It also helped to reduce these dangers and risks.

To protect the land from attack the king gave parts of the land to trusted lords. In return, they promised to fight to defend the king's land. If people wanted safety and defence, they had to live within the confines of the manor. Each manor was self-sufficient for food, clothes and weapons. Self-sufficiency was very important at that time because, if people were not able to grow food for themselves, there was no other way for them to get it.

The feudal system worked well, because it catered for everyone's essential needs such as protection and food. For slaves it was a very harsh life and if they were born within the manor, they would probably stay there their whole life. They had no right to do anything except work for their lord and so paid highly for the right to live and grow crops on the lord's land.

At least half the working week was spent on the land belonging to the lord and the church. Time might also be spent doing other work for the community such as clearing land, cutting firewood and building roads and bridges. The rest of the time the villagers were free to work their own land.

Over the next century or so Roger de Ramis's Bradfield properties were handed down through his family. His eldest son William died in 1130 and his estates then passed to his sons Roger and Richard. However, by 1086 Roger de Poitou had already had all of his holdings confiscated, perhaps for supporting William's son, Robert of Normandy, and in 1102 went into permanent exile. Possibly the small holding that he held in Bradfield was transferred to Roger de Ramis by 1086 explaining why Domesday states that it no longer existed then.

William de Ramis gave the patronage of the church to the Prior and Convent of St Bartholomew's in Smithfield, London sometime between 1175 and 1179. St Lawrence's first recorded vicar was Adam who was succeeded in 1224 by Walter.

Such detailed information as that provided by the Domesday survey would never again be available for centuries. So, as we move forward, we can only glimpse what life in Bradfield was like during the Middle Ages from written references to Lords of the Manor and Church clergy.

Chapter 3

Medieval times

```
Some key historical dates:-

  • 1307   Edward II
  • 1327   Edward III
  • 1348   The Black Death
  • 1377   Richard II
  • 1399   Henry IV
```

The Brokesburnes

At the beginning of the 14th century the old feudal system was still in place, but by then there were more freemen who had raised themselves up through hard work and good husbandry.

Around 1300 William Franke of Harwich was lord of the manor of Bradfield. This title was passed in 1312 to John de Brokesburne who had married William Franke's daughter. The manor of Bradfield Manston had passed to Aubrey de Vere, the Earl of Oxford.

Whilst the trading of goods between villagers would no doubt have been part of everyday life, on 20 February 1320, Edward II granted by Charter to John de Brokesburne the right to hold a weekly market at Bradfield. This market was to be held at the manor every Tuesday throughout the year.

Weekly markets were the main way in which medieval people bought, sold or traded goods. Farmers and craftsmen from the countryside would take their goods into the towns and villages to sell at the markets. Shopkeepers in the towns had to shut their own shops on market days and sell from the stalls. Villagers from outside the towns would go to the markets and fairs to buy goods that they could not get locally. Peddlers also travelled from village to village selling goods from their carts and provided a source of news.

You can just imagine the excitement amongst Bradfield folk when this right was granted to them. There had been weekly markets in other towns and villages in the local area for many years. For example, the Manningtree weekly market gained its grant in 1238, Dovercourt in 1222, and Harwich and Great Oakley in 1253. Perhaps most surprising is that Wix had been granted the right to hold a weekly market by King John in 1204, some years before all these others. Bradfield villagers must have been very pleased that at last they could now hold their own market, more than a century after its nearest neighbour had received its grant.

By the same Charter, Edward II also granted John de Brokesburne permission to hold an annual fair "on the vigil, feast and morrow" of St Lawrence (i.e. 9, 10 and 11 of August) each year, again to be held at the manor.

Artist's impression of a medieval market such as could have been held in Bradfield from 1320. (Drawn by Henry Lambon)

The range of goods available at these annual fairs was much larger than at the local markets and probably included goods from other countries. The Crusades had created much more interest in foreign goods and merchants from the East were welcomed to sell fine clothes, wines, spices and lace. One of the largest fairs in England was the Stourbridge fair held near Cambridge after the September harvest. This sometimes lasted for as long as five weeks. Although the Bradfield fair would obviously have been on a much smaller scale it would, nevertheless, have been one of the highlights of the year for villagers. These fairs would no doubt have been full of great joy and merriment.

The Black Death

In 1348, however, the mood of the villagers would have changed dramatically. News would probably have reached the village in early autumn of a deadly disease that was spreading across Europe.

It is not clear exactly when or where the Black Death reached England but it was probably sometime between late June and early August.

Over the next two years the disease killed about a third of the entire population. Given that the pre-plague population of England was in the range of 5-6 million people, fatalities may have reached as high as 2 million.

We can only guess how the Black Death affected Bradfield. Undoubtedly the

> ## The Black Death
>
> In 1347 a ship from Caffa, on the Black Sea, came ashore at Messina, Sicily. The crew of the ship, the few who were left alive, carried with them a disease so virulent that it could kill in a matter of hours. The Black Death was a bacteria-born disease and spread rapidly across the known world.

village would not have escaped the plague and there would have been long term economic difficulties for villagers. It is believed that Stephen Abbott was vicar of St Lawrence at the time of the Black Death and that in 1352 Alexander de Hanne succeeded him, but we have no idea of the exact dates or reasons for the change. Probably Stephen Abbott would have ministered to dying villagers, but whether he himself succumbed to the plague we will never know.

After the Black Death the nature of the economy changed to meet the changing social conditions. Land that had once been farmed was now given over to pasturing, which was much less labour-intensive. With the fall in population most landowners were not getting the rental income they needed, and were forced to lease their land.

Peasants benefited through increased employment options and higher wages. Society became more mobile as peasants moved to accept work where they could command a good wage.

The short term economic prosperity did not last, however, and by the mid-15th century standards of living had fallen again. Yet for most people the Black Death represented a massive upheaval, one that changed the face of English society in a profound way.

The Brokesburne "dynasty"	
	Owned manor from
William Franke	c1300
John de Brokesburne	1312
Robert de Brokesburne	1342
Margery de Brokesburne	1343
Edmund de Brokesburne	1385

John de Brokesburne died in 1342 and the manor passed to his son Robert, from his first marriage. In 1331 John had married for a second time and his new wife, Margery, bore him a son, Edmund in 1340 who was just two when his father died. Within a year or so of Robert de Brokesburne inheriting Bradfield, he decided to renounce his title and granted the manor to his stepmother Margery and her male heirs of John de Brokesburne. It is not known why Robert decided to give up his entitlement, but it has been suggested that he may have been renouncing this world and its wealth and about to go into a monastery.

On Margery's death in 1385, Edmund de Brokesburne inherited Bradfield manor, became MP for Essex in 1386 and in 1396 was granted "free warren" (i.e. the right to kill game of certain species) by Richard II over all his lands in Bradfield, Mistley, Wrabness, Ramsey, Dovercourt and Wix. Edmund was a military man and from the beginning of Richard II's reign had figured on Royal commissions. The most notable of these was for the defence of Harwich in case of attack from France.

It appears that Edmund did not have a male heir. His daughter by his first wife married Sir William Rainsford and in 1397 ownership of the manor at Bradfield transferred to the Rainsford family.

1400 – 1560

The Rainsfords

> Some key historical dates:-
>
> - 1413 Henry V
> - 1422 Henry VI
> - 1461 Edward IV
> - 1483 Edward V
> - 1483 Richard III
> - 1485 Henry VII
> - 1509 Henry VIII
> - 1534 Reformation of the Church
> - 1536 Dissolution of the monasteries starts
> - 1547 Edward VI – Parish records start
> - 1553 Mary
> - 1559 Elizabeth I

After the Brokesburnes, the Rainsford family held the manor at Bradfield for more than 100 years. Sir William Rainsford passed it to his son Sir Lawrence Rainsford and he to his son Sir John Rainsford (Snr).

Sir John Rainsford (Snr) was knighted by Henry VII. He served as a captain in the French wars under Henry VII and Henry VIII and was rewarded for his services with grants of lands and privileges. His son and namesake also led an active military career.

Sir John Rainsford (Jnr) was born around 1482 and married Elizabeth, the only daughter of Edward Knyvett, an extensive landowner in East Anglia. When Knyvett died soon after, he left the greater part of his lands in trust for Elizabeth's stepmother Catherine for life. This settlement greatly reduced Rainsford's prospects and expectations.

On his father's death, about the end of 1521, Rainsford again had to endure the elaborate provision made for his stepmother and his two sisters, one of whom married Sir Thomas Darcy, a ward of his father's and a notable beneficiary in the will. Sir William Waldegrave (c1507-1554) married Julian Rainsford, Sir John Rainsford's other daughter in 1528.

In 1523 Rainsford was knighted for his part in the capture of Morlaix on the north-west coast of France in the previous year. During the Hundred Years War Morlaix was held by the French and the English in turn, and was retaken by the English in 1522.

The Rainsford "dynasty"	
	Owned manor from
Sir William Rainsford	c1420
Sir Lawrence Rainsford	c1450
Sir John Rainsford (Snr)	1490
Sir John Rainsford (Jnr)	1521

Rainsford led a turbulent life and was twice charged with murder, once in 1511 when he was tried in the King's Bench. No details can be found, but according to House of Commons records he was either acquitted or pardoned.

About ten years later he was charged with a second murder. This time he was accused by Richard Vynes, who was an ex-servant of the abbot of Colchester. For some unknown reason Vynes had fallen out with Rainsford's father (Sir John Rainsford Snr) and it was thought that as a result he held a grudge against the whole Rainsford family. He accused Rainsford of committing a murder within the sanctuary of Colchester Abbey. Vynes claimed to have seen Rainsford kill a man in the abbey grounds and he was discovered with the body. Rainsford's answer to the accusation was that he had been talking to the victim when two men entered and killed him after a struggle. Rainsford's efforts to protect him failed because he was unarmed at the time. Not realising the seriousness of his wounds, Rainsford had tried to help the man which explained why he was found with the body. It seems that all the evidence was circumstantial and Rainsford was accordingly acquitted. Perhaps Vynes really did hold some sort of grudge as he also charged Rainsford with having harboured amongst his staff a tailor who had previously committed a murder in London.

Guilty or not on these occasions, Rainsford seems to have been of a violent disposition and was described by a neighbour of his as "a very dangerous man of his hands and one that delighteth much in beating, mayheming and evil entreating your subjects".

It is thought that the Rainsfords built Bradfield Hall in the early 1500s. This early Tudor building survived for several hundred years, but was eventually demolished in 1955.

Rainsford's time at Bradfield saw the rise of the Protestant movement across Europe that resulted in the Reformation of the Church. The reason for this change of religious mood was primarily theological in Europe. By contrast in England it was largely political, following the Pope's refusal to allow Henry VIII to divorce Catherine of Aragon, and resulted in Henry setting himself up as the head of the Church of England. In 1526, with the consent of Bishop Tunstall, Rainsford removed the Holy Communion "host" from St Lawrence Church to a specially built chapel at Bradfield Hall so that it would be safe from desecration. Some churches in the area had been desecrated by Protestant activists and Rainsford presumably wanted to protect Bradfield's church. According to the list of vicars in St Lawrence church, Thomas Hornsay became vicar in that year taking over from Giles Wright. Perhaps there was some dispute about the host's removal from the church which resulted in the change in stewardship.

In 1529 Rainsford became Member of Parliament for Colchester. Despite having been charged with murder twice, and being of a violent disposition, Rainsford seems to have had a lot of friends in high places.

At Bradfield Manston there was a nunnery in medieval times, which was a daughter house to the Abbey at Wix with a chapel dedicated to "Our Lady in the Oats". At the dissolution of the monasteries (1536-41) Sir John Rainsford acquired the property and gave it to his son Jakys, hence Jacques Hall as it is today.

In 1539 Rainsford was busy preparing the Essex coastal defences against the expected invasion by the French. He had raised a hundred men for the king at the time of the Northern rebellion, and had been among those summoned to the christening of Prince Edward in October 1537 and the wedding reception of Anne of Cleves two years later.

Henry VIII visited Bradfield in the summer of 1541 and stayed with Rainsford at Bradfield Hall.

On 30 June 1541, Henry VIII, half of his privy councillors (the other half were left in London to govern), his royal household and an entourage of 4-5,000 horsemen (as well as hangers on), left Hampton Court for York. His main objective was to meet with James V of Scotland. He and his entourage took nearly three months to travel to York, stopping at various places along the way. They finally arrived in York on 16 September. After waiting in vain for James to arrive for nine days in York, Henry returned to London on 24 October.

On his way up to York it is known that Henry stayed at Lincoln (9 August), Scooby in Nottinghamshire (17 August) and Pontefract (23 August).

Sometime probably around mid to late July 1541, therefore, Henry must have visited Bradfield. With him was his fifth wife, Catherine Howard whom he had married less than a year earlier. A few months prior to their departure for York Catherine embarked on a romance with Henry's favourite courtier, Thomas Culpeper and they met again on the King's "progress" to York. Henry eventually found out about Catherine's affair with Culpeper and she was charged with treason. Culpeper was hung, drawn and quartered on 10 December 1541 and Catherine was beheaded on 13 February 1542.

After Henry VIII's death in 1547 Rainsford remained in favour under Edward VI and died within a year of Elizabeth I's succession in 1559.

With his death ended the Rainsford dynasty at Bradfield.

Although we have little knowledge of the residents of Bradfield at this time we do a have couple of interesting extracts from two wills from 1581 and 1582:-

John Churchman, 1581

To Grace Martin a young cow and four ewes.

To my daughter Alice a cow, she to choose it, also 10s a year to be paid by my wife as long as she live. One great kettle and pot.

To my sister's son Wm. Grene, a cow and a ewe.

To my wife four horses and an axe to give or to sell at her pleasure also forty-eight sheep, to my daughter after her death.

To Alice a feather bed, a great kettle and a brass pot after my wife decease.

Henry Allman, 1582

To the poor 6s 8d.

To my brother Th. Allman 10s, my petticoat, my russet jerkin.

To my good wife my mortar.

To John Coper 12d.

My house and lands, called Kent, to be sold and the money to my three children part and part alike. Philip and Simon at twenty-one and my daughter Mary at eighteen.

1560-1700

The Grimstons

Some key historical dates:-

- 1603   James I
- 1625   Charles I
- 1642   Civil War
- 1649   Charles I executed and "Commonwealth" declared
- 1651   Second Civil War
- 1658   Cromwell dies
- 1660   Charles II
- 1685   James II
- 1688   William & Mary
- 1696   Act to establish workhouses

In 1568 William Waldegrave was lord of the manor of Bradfield Hall but soon after that date it passed to John Harbottle. Harbottle had a daughter, Joan, who married Thomas Risby of Lavenham. Joan Risby died in 1589 and there is a full length brass of her in the church.

In 1577 John Harbottle died and is buried at Bradfield (there is a small brass in St Lawrence Church). His grand-daughter, also named Joan after her mother, married Edward Grimston in 1589. So started the next one hundred years of Bradfield history - the Grimston dynasty. Grimston claimed to be directly descended from Sylvester, William the Conquerer's standard bearer.

Edward Grimston was born in 1507. In 1553 he became MP for Eye and was also appointed Comptroller of Calais. Calais had been under British rule since 1347 when the town was besieged and captured by Edward III. Grimston had a long and distinguished service both militarily, being an expert in national defence (he was a member of the Bodyguard of Spears in 1539), and politically.

Upon his appointment as Comptroller of Calais he was critical of the town's defences. Indeed the town was captured by the Duke of Guise five years later. Grimston was taken prisoner and sent to the Bastille in Paris. It appears that incarceration in the Bastille was no match for Grimston. The story goes that he escaped within two years. Apparently he procured a file and gradually wore through the window bars, let himself down with a rope and swapped clothes with his servant waiting on the other end.

HERE LYETH IOANE RYSBYE THE WIFE OF THOMAS RYSBYE CENT: DAVGHTER AND HEIRE OF IOHN HARBOTTELL ESQ: SHE LIVED IN THE FEARE OF GOD AND DIED IN THE FAITH OF CHRIST IN OCTOBER ANO DNI 1598. ÆTATIS SVA 1 X

Brass of Joan Risby

PLATE 16 — EDWARD GRIMSTON OF GRAY'S INN (BUT SEE PAGE 35

Edward Grimston

On his return to England he was charged with high treason but was acquitted. His parliamentary career was notable and he represented Ipswich and other Suffolk constituencies. In 1593, at the age of 86, he was still making speeches in the House of Commons as MP for Orford. He was an amazing man and engaged in diplomatic work in France in 1582 and 1587. He died aged 92 in Ipswich in 1599 and was buried at Rishangles near Eye.

Joan and Edward Grimston christened their son Harbottle after Joan's grandfather, and following Edward's death the estate transferred to Harbottle.

Sir Harbottle Grimston (c. 1569–1648) was Bradfield's first Baronet and, like his father before him, he had a distinguished political career. He was a member of the House of Commons at various times between 1626 and 1648 and was a supporter of the Parliamentarian side in the English Civil War. He was created Baronet of Bradfield on 25 November 1611 and in 1614 he was appointed High Sheriff of Essex.

In 1626 Grimston was elected Member of Parliament for Essex. He was re-elected in 1628 and held the seat until 1629 when King Charles decided to rule without parliament for 11 years. In April 1640 he was re-elected MP for Essex in the Short Parliament. In November 1640 he was elected MP for Harwich in

Sir Harbottle Grimston 1st Baronet

the Long Parliament. He held the seat until his death in 1648.

It is said that Grimston's ghost, seated on a white horse, still haunts the churchyard. The story is that the horse was interred in the churchyard at the same time as its master.

Tombstone of Sir Harbottle Grimston 1st Baronet in St Lawrence Church

24

Grimston married Elizabeth Coppenger, daughter of Ralph Coppenger of Stoke in Kent. They had five sons and the second, who was also called Harbottle, succeeded to the baronetcy.

Sir Harbottle Grimston 2nd Baronet

Sir Harbottle Grimston, 2nd Baronet (27 January 1603 – 2 January 1685) was born at Bradfield Hall and educated at Emmanuel College, Cambridge.

He became a barrister at Lincoln's Inn and was appointed Recorder of Harwich and Recorder of Colchester. Grimston was MP for Colchester in the 1640s, during which time he attacked the Archbishop of Canterbury (Archbishop Laud) vigorously for his high church dogma and also his opposition to land enclosure legislation. As a landowner Grimston may have already "enclosed" his lands and would be opposed to any anti-enclosure legislation. He was also a member of important parliamentary committees.

He did not like taking up arms against the king but remained nominally a supporter of the Parliamentary party during the Civil War. He was president of the committee which investigated the escape of the king from Hampton Court in 1647 and was one of those who negotiated with Charles I at Newport in 1648, when he is said to have fallen on his knees and urged the king to come to terms.

From this time Grimston's sympathies appear to have changed and been with the Royalists. Turned out of the House of Commons when the Royalists were expelled, he was imprisoned. He was, however, released after promising to do nothing detrimental to the parliament or the army, and spent the next few years in retirement. Before this time, his elder brother having already died, he had succeeded his father as Bradfield's 2nd baronet. In 1656 he was returned to Oliver Cromwell's second parliament as member for Essex but he was not allowed to take his seat and, with 97 others who were similarly treated, he issued a "remonstrance" (protest) to the public complaining of his exclusion.

The Grimston "dynasty"	
	Owned manor from
William Waldegrave	c1560
John Harbottle	c1570
Edward Grimston	1577
Sir Harbottle Grimston (1st Baronet)	1610
Sir Harbottle Grimston (2nd Baronet)	1647
William Luckyn	1684

He was among the members who re-entered parliament in February 1660, was then a member of the Council of State, and was chosen Speaker of the House of Commons later that year. As Speaker he visited Charles II at Breda, and addressed him in very flattering terms on his return to London. He only held this post, however, for a few months from April to December in 1660.

Grimston was a Justice of the Peace for Essex between 1639 and 1648 and, during his period of office, he presided over a number of cases brought to court by the self-proclaimed Witchfinder General, Matthew Hopkins. Hopkins was born in 1620 and between 1644 and his early death three years later, engaged in witch hunts throughout East Anglia. He lived in Manningtree and is believed to have been responsible for the deaths of 300 women (and some men) for witchcraft between 1644 and 1646. His campaign was ferocious. This is an amazing total in such a short period, bearing in mind that it has been estimated that witch trials in the whole of England during the 15th to 18th centuries resulted in fewer than 500 executions. In all the cases presided over by Grimston all defendants were found innocent.

Grimston did not retain the office of Speaker in the next parliament, but he was a member of the commission that tried those responsible for the death of Charles I and, in November 1660, he was appointed Master of the Rolls (i.e. responsible for the records of the Chancery Court), a post that he held for nearly 25 years until January 1685.

According to Parliamentary archives in June 1648 Grimston's house, Bradfield Hall, was occupied in his absence by a party of troops belonging to the army of the Earl of Warwick, who plundered it and turned out his wife. The Earl of Warwick (Robert Rich, 2nd Earl, 1587–1658) was an extremely powerful landowner with estates in Essex and London and interests in the colonies. He was a staunch Puritan and Parliament had appointed him Lord High Admiral in March 1642. Warwick and Grimston knew each other – Warwick had presided over the Chelmsford Witch trials of Matthew Hopkins in 1645 at which Grimston appeared as JP. They were nominally on the same side but Warwick seems to have been an extremist whereas Grimston comes across as a moderate, eager to negotiate, possibly a fence-sitter.

It is hard to believe that Warwick would have been personally involved in the sack of Bradfield Hall. There was constant infighting in the Parliamentarian ranks at this time and bands of militia were going about the country committing lawless acts, even atrocities, and the "party of troops" may have had only a loose connection to the Earl's army. It seems likely that the Grimstons preferred to live at their other estates after these traumatic events, and they lost interest in Bradfield. Lady Grimston, in particular, might have been unwilling to go back to a house where she had suffered indignities at the hands of marauding soldiers.

After his death, Grimston's properties passed to his grand-nephew, William Luckyn, who was MP for St Albans. After he inherited Luckyn assumed the name of Grimston. His properties passed through his family line and one of his descendants was made Earl of Verulam.

Chapter 4

Changing rural scene

Some key historical dates:-

- 1702   Anne
- 1714   George I
- 1727   George II
- 1760   George III
- 1820   George IV
- 1830   William IV
- 1836   Tithe Commutation Act
- 1837   Victoria

By the late 1700s much of Bradfield was owned by Richard Rigby Jnr. He owned Bradfield Hall, Nether Hall and many other smaller properties. The Rigbys were a family of rich linen merchants and Richard Rigby Snr moved to Mistley in around 1720 with grand plans and, along with his son, set them in motion. Amongst their many ambitious plans, Richard's father commissioned Robert Adam in 1776 to redesign the church of St Mary the Virgin at Mistley, which had been built in 1735 (now demolished). This he did by adding the twin towers that still stand today.

The late 1700s marked a major turning point in British history which brought about changes in agriculture, manufacturing, mining, transportation and technology that had a profound effect on the social, economic and cultural conditions of the times.

A change that affected land ownership was in the way that tithe payments could be made. The payment of one tenth of local produce to the church had been established in Anglo-Saxon times, before the Norman Conquest. This payment was originally in kind - every tenth "stook" of corn, for example - and it originally supported the local priest. Tithes themselves were controversial, particularly

28

among non-conformists who resented supporting the established church, and payment in kind was not convenient for either the farmer or the tithe owner.

The Tithe Commutation Act 1836 established a process by which tithes could be converted to money payments. This required the drawing of an accurate map (the accuracy of which was certified by commissioners) showing all the land in the parish. The series of maps resulting from this legislation provides unprecedented coverage, detail and accuracy.

In 1841 the detailed tithe map of Bradfield was drawn up so that each landowner's payment could be calculated and converted into money payments. It is a fascinatingly detailed document. In 1841, included amongst the major landowners in Bradfield were Edward Norman, Thomas Partridge and James Hardy.

The most significant change in rural life was, however, as a result of the introduction of steam power. Not only did this revolutionise manufacturing but also farming methods. The impact of this change on society was enormous, but perhaps the biggest advance as far as the residents of Bradfield were concerned, was the arrival of the railway.

The Railway

It is very difficult for us, living in the 21st century with all the modern advancements in travel and communication, to imagine just how life-changing the coming of the railways would have been to our Victorian ancestors.

Before the railway most people, especially the poor, travelled very little. To travel even a few miles by coach was both expensive and time consuming. Goods and services were mostly provided locally. The building of the railways changed all this by creating jobs, making goods cheaper, speeding up the spread of information and changing the countryside in a way that neither the canals nor roads had been able to.

The railway also changed the time that people lived by. Before the railways each part of the country had its own time, based on local daylight hours. Trains travelled much faster than any other means of transport had ever done and a consistent time system was needed in order for the railways to operate properly. In 1880 London Greenwich Mean Time became everyone's time in Britain.

The railways spread rapidly. In 1825 there were only 25 miles of railway in the U.K. By 1875 this had grown to 160,000 miles! The main period of "railway mania" was from 1843 to 1850 and it was soon after this that the railway arrived in Bradfield.

One of the many railway companies to be established during this period was the Eastern Counties Railway in 1839. Initially it built a railway from Mile End in East London to Romford, but this was soon extended out to Colchester. In 1843 the E.C.R. applied for permission to build a line from Colchester to Harwich but this was refused by Parliament. Four years later a separate company, the Eastern Union Railway, which ran the railway from Colchester to Ipswich, was authorised to build a branch line from Manningtree to Harwich, but the company's financial troubles delayed work until 1853. When the line was finally opened the E.C.R. had taken over the E.U.R. and in 1862 it too was merged into what became the Great Eastern Railway.

Bradfield Station in the early 1900s

The first train reached Harwich on 4 August 1854 and the first passenger train on 15 August amid great celebration from thousands of local people and railway representatives and shareholders. Although the line was opened in 1854 Bradfield station was not built until 1856.

There were eight stops along the line starting at Manningtree, then Mistley and then Bradfield station. The next stop was Priory Halt (near Wrabness), then Wrabness, Parkeston Quay, Dovercourt Bay and finally Harwich station.

The Mistley, Thorpe and Walton Railway Company

In 1863 the Mistley, Thorpe and Walton Railway Company was established which was to provide a link with Ipswich and the North. The line was planned to pass through Mistley, Bradfield, Wix, Beaumont, Thorpe, Kirby, Great Holland, Frinton and then on to Walton. Nine bridges were planned and two railway stations, one of which was to be at Bradfield, near Bradfield Hall. Work commenced in 1864, but from the outset the project went badly.

Delays caused so many amendments to the schedule that the constructor was dismissed, but refused to quit the site until forcibly driven out. There were then money problems and in 1868 work ceased and the following year the line was abandoned altogether and the company wound up. At the closure of the company the line had reached Tendring and six bridges had been, or were in the process of being constructed but neither of the two stations had been built. Remnants of this aborted project, which ran between Dovehouse Farm and Whitehouse Farm and down to the west of Bradfield Hall, still remain to this day.

Railway Accident

The Manningtree to Harwich branch line had been open just short of ten years when a serious accident occurred near Jacques Hall, Bradfield in July 1864. The accident was significant enough to be reported in The Illustrated London News on 23 July 1864, together with the following illustration:-

It should, perhaps, be noted that this illustration bears absolutely no resemblance to Bradfield or its surrounding areas and was probably totally imaginative. Also the track gauge appears to be several feet wider than it should be!

The full report in The Illustrated London News read as follows:-

"One of our Illustrations represents the serious accident which took place at Bradfield, in Essex, on Wednesday week, by the overthrow of the up-train which started from Harwich at 2.55 pm, on the Great Eastern Railway. The train is run in connection with the new line of Rotterdam steamers which ply from Harwich. When it had proceeded on its journey towards London as far as within half a mile of Bradfield Station, the engine lurched over and crashed down the sharp embankment, dragging all the train after it. The position of the train is shown in our Engraving, which is from a sketch by one of the passengers. The stoker was killed on the spot, having been crushed by the engine. He lay with his hand still grasping the metal handle of the break. The driver, who also stayed at his post, escaped. The passengers, in the greatest alarm, got out of the carriages as they best could, and helped those who were injured; and it was some time before it was ascertained that, although several persons had been cut, bruised and injured, some severely, only the stoker had been killed. An inquest has been opened upon the body of the stoker. The Rector of Bradfield sent those who were most hurt to the rectory-house where they were cared for in the kindest manner, and their wounds attended to. The passengers who were able to proceed, after a delay of

about four hours, were brought to town by a train which was dispatched for the purpose."

By the late 1800s there were six or seven trains a day in each direction on the branch line and three or four on Sundays. Here is an extract from the Mistley-cum-Bradfield Parish Magazine in 1889 which shows the times of the trains from Mistley.

TRAIN SERVICE FROM MISTLEY.

To Manningtree—8.27, 10.22, 1.29, 3.44, 6.10, 8.44.
To Harwich—7.12, 9.3, 11.45, 2.3, 4.40, 7.14, 11.14.

SUNDAYS

To Manningtree—9.34, 5.27, 10.29.
To Harwich—10.30, 4.34, 6.6, 11.11.

All these, with the exception of the 11.14 p.m. train, stop at Bradfield to take up or set down passengers. The 6.55 from Manningtree, and the 8.10 from Harwich, together with the Sunday trains (excepting the 11.11 p.m.) only stop if required. Notice must be given to the Guard at the preceding stopping station.

Today there are only six stops. Priory Halt closed when the mine depot closed in the late 1960s, and Bradfield station closed in 1956 and was demolished in 1986. Among the reasons for the Bradfield station closure was the lack of passenger traffic and the fact that, unlike the other smaller stations along this line such as Mistley and Wrabness, Bradfield never had goods traffic. Mistley and Wrabness were hives of industry, where almost anything was delivered for the customer to pick up.

Chapter 5

Bradfield in 1881

At this stage in our history of Bradfield it might be interesting to pause and take a more detailed look at the people and life of the village. In 1875 the Ordnance Survey produced its first large scale map of Bradfield. At a scale of one mile to 25 inches it provides in fascinating detail all of the buildings, even down to showing which gardens had wells and which neighbours would have shared them. The national census carried out in 1881 provides details of the 800+ residents of Bradfield including their age, occupation and place of birth.

Using these two valuable information sources this chapter of our book takes a circular trip around Bradfield in 1881 looking at the people and buildings of the village to try to get a flavour of what rural village life was like in mid-Victorian Essex. At that time the village was centred around the church, pub, shop and businesses of The Street up to Mill Lane.

It is hard for us today to fully appreciate how different life must have been in Victorian times. We are used to travel, communication and interaction across a hugely larger scale than would have been the case in 1881. We do not depend so heavily on the village to supply our needs. For example, we travel to a supermarket to buy goods produced all over the UK and further afield. In 1881 things would have been very different. Apart from a few specialist goods all of the village's produce and services would have been provided from within the community. As such there would have been a much stronger community spirit amongst people who were, in effect, all in the same boat. If the harvest was poor, then everyone in the village would be affected. Therefore everyone would be pulling together to make things work.

Another major difference between now and then is that in 1881 over 95% of villagers were either born in Bradfield or within a radius of perhaps 20 or so miles of Bradfield. Also, whilst the population has not grown dramatically in the last century or so (from about 800 to 1,100), the number of houses has more than doubled. As will be seen, family sizes were much larger than today and there were many instances where more than five people lived in what were then small dwellings.

Mortality rates were much higher then, of course, and villagers would perhaps, as a consequence, have been much more religious and many would have gone regularly to one of the village churches.

There was a good postal and rail service by 1881, which would have given villagers some freedoms not previously enjoyed, but there was, of course, no electricity, gas or telephone, let alone radio, television or the internet.

As we travel around the village it will be seen that a very large proportion of male adults were agricultural labourers who would have worked on one of the many village farms. Most of the land surrounding the village was arable with the chief crops being wheat, barley and oats. Life in the fields would have been hard work from spring to autumn particularly and there would have been even greater hardships during the winter months.

In 1881 Bradfield was distinctly two villages – Bradfield (Street) and Bradfield Heath. There were few buildings between the two, unlike today where new homes built in the last century have filled in much of the road in between resulting in the unified village we have today.

We start our journey around the village at The Street end and then travel clockwise round to Bradfield Heath and then up and along the river ending at Jacques Hall.

(The Ordnance Survey maps set out in the next section of the book are all reproduced by courtesy of Essex Record Office).

1875 map of the Bradfield Street end of the village

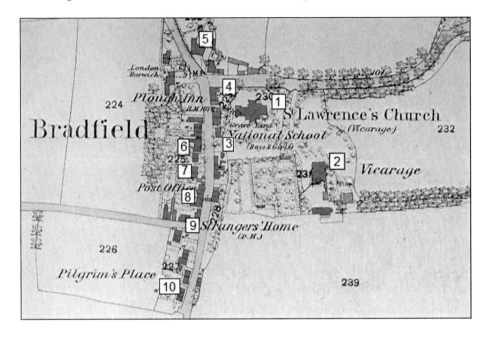

St Lawrence Church (1 on map)

The village's parish church is by far and away Bradfield's oldest surviving building. The church's patron saint, Lawrence, was born around 225 AD. He was one of the seven deacons of ancient Rome who were killed during the persecution of Valerian in 258 AD. Valerian heard rumours that the Christian church had hoards of treasure and he wanted it for himself. He summoned Lawrence, who was keeper of the church books, to tell him how much treasure there was and where it could be found. Lawrence showed the emperor two books. The first was accounts stating that everything received had been distributed and the other a list of all the souls in the church's care (the poor, sick, orphaned, etc) and said that this was the treasure of the church. Valerian showed his displeasure by ordering Lawrence and his books to be roasted on a gridiron.

St Lawrence Church in about 1910

The current building, with its many changes and restorations over the centuries, dates back to the 1200s, but now the roof and windows contain only a small amount of work from this early date and the walls are covered with cement and plaster. However, it is thought that there was a much older building beneath the current foundations. It can be seen that the church tower is not aligned with the main body of the church. This seems rather odd and in 1958, when the floor around the altar was being re-laid, a line of foundations was discovered underneath that was on the same axis as the tower, so it is highly probable that an earlier building existed, perhaps of Anglo-Saxon origin.

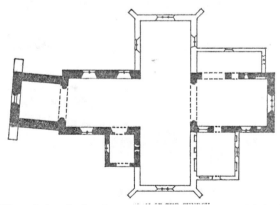
Plan of church showing misalignment of tower with body of the church

Apart from the tower, this original structure would have been demolished and a new church built, which for some unknown reason, was constructed at a slight angle to the tower and the original building. A south door entrance and porch was added in the 1300s. Unlike the current flat-topped tower, a few centuries ago there was a steeple pointing proudly towards the heavens. In 1633 it was recorded that "the steeple wants pargeting without and within the belfry" and by 1683 "the steeple is much decayed in the lower part". By 1707 the steeple had fallen down and it appears that all villagers were expected to pay towards its replacement - "the churchwarden is admonished to make a rate of 12d in the pound and collect the same and certify thereof at next Easter visitation and then present all that refuse to pay to it".

The only evidence we can find of how the replacement church steeple once looked is from a painting by Revd. John Louis Petit, which is thought to have been made in the 1830s, shortly before the church's transepts were built. John Louis Petit was born in Ashton-under-Lyne, Lancashire in 1801 of French Huguenot parents who were originally from Caen. His schooling began at Eton and finished at Trinity College, Cambridge where he was a scholar. Petit was ordained in 1824 and become the curate of Bradfield. However, he soon retired

Painting of St Lawrence Church in about 1830.

from parochial duties and moved to Shropshire. Petit died in 1868. It is likely that he painted this picture whilst he was living in Bradfield.

Much rebuilding and restoration has taken place over the years of which the most significant was in 1840, when the steeple was taken down and the height of the tower increased by bricks as can be seen today. The transepts were also added in 1840 and the porch restored.

The oldest visible feature of the church that visitors can see today is the font, which is currently positioned in the tower, and may date from the 1100s. This font has possibly been used for baptisms in Bradfield for nearly 900 years!

St Lawrence Church's font

Whilst the font may be the oldest feature of the church, the second oldest cannot be seen, but will on occasions be heard. The church has one bell that was made in the 1300s. It has an inscription that is partly in English and partly in Latin –

"I AM KOC OF THIS FLOC WIT GLORIA TIBI DOMINE".

[I am cock of this flock, Glory be to Thee O Lord]

The "floc" is believed to be the set of bells and not the worshippers. In September 1552 an inventory of the church was taken and the commissioners noted that there were originally three bells, but Sir John Rainsford, lord of the parish, "had away" with the two biggest, so that only one remains in the church. We have no idea what Rainsford did with the two bells he took, but we have already seen earlier in this book that he seems to have been rather a law unto himself.

There are many plaques and stones in the church in memory of notable villagers over the years, in particular the Grimston family and parish vicars (including a full list of vicars and patrons of the church). Much could be written about the church, but space in this short history prevents this. In 1962 a booklet was published by the Revd. Denis Bayley "Bradfield Church Essex and Notes on the Grimston Family at Bradfield". Although now long out of print there are copies that the reader might borrow if interested in learning more about Bradfield's parish church. Bayley was President of the Essex Archaeological Society and his booklet is a very thorough learned study of the church's and the Grimston family's history.

St Lawrence has some fine stained glass windows. The window in the wall behind the altar is in memory of the Revd. Leighton George Hayne and was provided by parishioners in the late 1880s and those in the south transept were commissioned by Walter Buchanan Nichols of Stour Lodge in memory of his two sons who died during the First World War. The windows in the north transept are in memory of Dame Hannah Louise Dunning who died in December 1914 and the two more modern windows on the north side of the nave were designed in 1960 by Miss Rosemary Rutherford, a Suffolk artist who designed stained glass windows for many churches in East Anglia and further afield. The Rutherford windows were given by Miss Martha Louisa Dunning.

There are a number of significant memorials/graves in the churchyard. One in particular, in addition to the Hayne and Dunning memorials mentioned later in this book, is a grave tucked away in the south-east corner of the graveyard containing the remains of George Forbes. Forbes was born in 1825 and moved from Aberdeen to join the Bank of England in 1844 at the age of 19. He worked at the Bank for a total of 28 years and was Chief Cashier from 1866-1873. He suffered from poor health during his time as Chief Cashier and sadly had to resign his office on 30 June 1873 at the young age of 48. In his resignation letter to the Bank he said "I am grateful for the large indulgence granted to me during my long illness". He died less than a year later at Mistley Abbey on 25 May 1874.

£5 notes signed by George Forbes

George Forbes was the 13th Chief Cashier and the first to have his signature printed on bank notes, a tradition that continues to the present day. During his first few years as Chief Cashier the Bank's notes were signed by other officers at the Bank (either printed or handwritten), but on 1st November 1870 this practice changed and from that date all bank notes bear the printed signature of the Chief Cashier. £5 and £10 notes bearing George Forbes' printed signature exist, but are extremely rare and a copy in good condition would today probably fetch in excess of £15,000.

The Vicarage (2 on map)

Conveniently built next to the church was The Vicarage (now Bradfield Place). In 1881 the Revd. Leighton George Hayne (then aged 45) was vicar of St Lawrence and lived there with his wife Agnes (50) and their teenage son Richard.

The Revd. Leighton Hayne

Hayne was a Doctor of Music and had then been vicar for ten years. He died just two years later and is buried in the churchyard where there is a prominent memorial. There are also dedications in the church to him and his father, Revd. Richard Hayne.

Two servants lived with the Hayne family - Mary Dayman (27) was the cook and Elizabeth Fairweather (also 27) was housemaid. At the time of the census there was a visitor at the vicarage – Nathan Howlett. Although he was only 16 he was a teacher. Perhaps he was teaching temporarily at the village school.

The Revd. Leighton Hayne was, to say the least, a colourful character and rather eccentric. According to Denis Bayley's booklet of the church "it was about 1875 that many alterations were made in the church, the worst possible period for 'restoration' work", for which Hayne was responsible. These changes were made at about the same time that the Revd. Hayne brought his huge five-manual organ, which he acquired when he was in Oxford, to Bradfield. It is said that it took ten large railway trucks to transport the organ and its pipes to Bradfield, which he stored adjacent to the stables at the vicarage. The organ was too big to fit in the church, so undeterred he went ahead and built a second large organ which he thought would fit.

He is said to have wrought havoc in the chancel by trying to incorporate the organ in a small village church. To accommodate the new organ a chamber was built on the north side of the chancel and some of the wooden pipes were so huge that he placed them horizontally in a cavity under the chancel floor. All this work was carried out by Hayne himself with the help of village builder Francis Puxley who lived in Wix Road, in an atmosphere of secrecy and sometimes at night. The pipes under the floor were unsatisfactory and had to be removed. We can only guess at the reaction of villagers to some of Revd. Hayne's actions.

The vicarage was probably built around the middle of the 18th century and its first occupant was Revd. Charles Umfreville. He was born in 1700 and was Bradfield's longest serving vicar (47 years) from 1727 until his death in 1774. There is a memorial to him in the south transept of the church.

Surrounding the old vicarage is a "crinkle-crankle" (or "serpentine") brick wall possibly built at the same time as the vicarage. The crinkle crankle wall economises on bricks, despite its sinuous configuration, because it can be made just one brick thin. If a wall this thin was to be made in a straight line, without buttresses, it would easily topple over. The alternate convex and concave curves in the wall provide stability and help it to resist lateral forces. Many crinkle crankle walls are found in East Anglia, particularly in Suffolk.

Bradfield's "crinkle-crankle" wall

It has been suggested that there are two tunnels leading from the house which were used to smuggle brandy barrels. Another, less romantic, suggestion is that they may be "rainbacks" for taking rain water away from the house. A former owner recalls exploring the cellars with a party of friends and discovering two tunnels. Both tunnels started from a point outside the front door. An entrance porch was subsequently built over the spot. It is said that one tunnel travels towards the lych-gate and emerges into the centre of four cypress trees and the other goes in a north-westerly direction towards Harwich Road and halts below an apparently unnamed tomb.

National School (3 on map)

The National School in The Street was in front of the church and adjacent to where the lych gate now stands. It was built in 1841 at a cost of £140. Just ten years later it was already inadequate and was rebuilt in 1851 to accommodate 75 pupils.

The National School in about 1912 (the little girl is Annie Burrows who lived next door in Elderberry Cottage)

The Education Act passed just a year before the 1881 census made school attendance compulsory for all children aged between five and ten years and as a result an extra classroom for another 30 children was added in 1884. This was still insufficient and in 1898 the School Managers approved the building of yet another room, but it was never built. Instead, a "New Council School" was built in Heath Road supposedly to accommodate 200 pupils, and the National School closed in December 1906. The teaching staff and 128 pupils then transferred to the Council school which opened on 7 January 1907. The old school was subsequently used by various groups including the Sunday School and the Scouts until it was demolished about 1933.

Miss Catherine Newman (aged 24) was mistress at the National School in 1881. She was born in Ponders End in Middlesex and boarded at Bradfield Heath Farm.

Plough Inn (4 on map)

The Plough Inn

Situated on the corner of Harwich Road and The Street, the Plough Inn would have been in the heart of the village.

It has been suggested that the Plough provided fresh horses for the Post Chaise and London Stage coaches. This seems unlikely as there is no evidence of particularly big stables and, in those days, coaches turned off at Ship Hill and ran along the beach in order to avoid the hills between Bradfield and Wrabness. This old road has long since been eroded away by the tide.

Richard Good (58) was landlord of the Plough in 1881 and, according to the census, he was a Licensed Victualler and Agricultural Labourer. He lived with his wife Emma, 20 years his junior, and their two daughters Emily (13) and Eliza

(10). Three agricultural labourers also lodged at the Plough – Nathan Culf (42), Nathaniel Offord (47) and Benjamin Whittle (17).

At the end of World War I, the Plough was in a fairly dilapidated condition and was bought and demolished by Sir Edward Dunning to provide a site for the war memorial which was erected in 1919.

The cellars of the old pub remain beneath the memorial.

General Store (5 on map)

The general store at the Bradfield Street end of the village, where a whole variety of goods could be bought, was situated near the corner of what is now Station Road and Harwich Road (now Acacia House). In 1881 the store (grocers and drapery) was run by John Scott Bacon who also ran and lived at the village Post Office. A few years later Allen Large ran the store and here is an advert from the parish magazine in 1911 which illustrates the wealth of products and service that this shop brought to the village.

45

Allen Large's delivery van in the early 1900s

The Bakers (6 on map)

The village bakers was on the west side of The Street (now The Laurels) and was run by Jonathan Brewster (aged 47) in 1881. The census states that he was married but there is no reference to his wife living with him. He lived with his son Joseph (18) and Henry Gould (15) was his servant.

At the time of the census there was a visitor at the bakers – William Purkis (22) who was a harness maker.

The photo on the following page shows the bakers shop in 1907, which was then owned by Mr AP Saunders.

View of The Street showing the baker's shop

Shoe makers (7 on map)

If you needed shoes in 1881, then you would probably go to what is now Hallam Cottage. At that time there were two separate semi-detached cottages, rather than the knocked through detached cottage of today. It is thought that they were originally Huguenot weavers' cottages, built in 1672. According to the deeds of the house John Spink (aged 61) owned the property in 1881. However, according to the census he and his wife, Ann (46), lived at the Post Office. Spink was a shoemaker and he and his wife are buried in St Lawrence churchyard.

The Post Office (8 on map)

The Post Office was next to the old Strangers Home on the corner of The Street and Mill Lane. In 1881 John Scott Bacon (aged 55) was postmaster. He was also a draper and grocer to the village. He lived with his wife Mahala (62) and grand-daughter Eleanor Aldred (aged 3).

47

Henry Pryor (58), who was an agricultural labourer, also lived at the Post Office with his wife Sarah (58) and their daughter Mary (13).

Letters arrived from Manningtree at 7.45 am and were dispatched to Manningtree at 7 pm. The nearest money order office was in Manningtree.

The Strangers Home (9 on map)

Postcard of the old Strangers Home in about 1910

On the corner of The Street and Mill Lane stood the original Strangers Home public house.

The "strangers" in question were Huguenot refugees who fled from Europe for fear of persecution for their Protestant beliefs and this was their meeting place. Mainly from France and the lowlands of Europe, the Huguenots settled first in Colchester from where they spread to Thorpe-le-Soken and gradually to other villages in the Tendring peninsula. The Huguenots brought with them skills and crafts that were to be of great benefit to rural districts. The field at the rear of the present Strangers Home was the site of a Huguenot refugee camp. The cottages round about there were traditional Flemish weavers' houses.

The Strangers Home ceased to be a public house in the early 1900s, but it continued to be used for private occupation and for public social gatherings until around 1950. It was demolished, along with the adjoining cottages, slaughterhouse and butchers in about 1962. John M Winney was the village butcher in 1881.

Frederick Mason (29) was landlord of the Strangers Home in 1881. He lived there with his wife Hannah (30) and one year old son W Frederick as well as his brother Arthur Mason (22) who was a shoemaker (cordwainer). They retained a general domestic servant, Sarah King (14).

Several other people were also lodging at the Strangers Home - James Webb (80), James Dickerson (58) (agricultural labourer) and his wife and daughter, and John Childs (18) (agricultural labourer) together with his younger brother and sister.

Pilgrim's Place (10 on map)

Anthony Winney (50) lived here with his wife Naomi (44), their two sons (8 & 12) and daughter (6), and George Tweed (Winney's brother-in-law), aged 48.

Tweed was a Chelsea Pensioner. It may at first sight seem unlikely that a Chelsea Pensioner would be resident in Bradfield. However, historically there were two types of Chelsea Pensioners – in-pensioners and out-pensioners. Only senior ranking officers could become in-pensioners and be cared for at the Chelsea hospital. Lower ranking army veterans might qualify as out-pensioners, i.e. receive a pension, but reside elsewhere. George Tweed died at the Union Workhouse in Tendring in 1910.

Near Pilgrim's Place in The Street was once the site of the village pound. Most villages had a pound for stray cattle, pigs, geese, and other animals to be driven into and kept there at the expense of the owner, until such time as he paid a fine (the amount claimed by the person on whose land they had strayed, for damage done), and a fee to the pound keeper for feeding and watering the strays. If not claimed within a few weeks, the animals were driven to the nearest market and sold, the proceeds going to the impounder and pound-keeper.

Other houses in and around The Street

The census does not give exact addresses in many cases. At other unknown addresses in The Street the head of the household in most cases was an agricultural labourer, but some had other occupations:-

Abraham Fox (64) - shop porter
William Durrant (70) - carpenter
John Marshall (49) - market gardener
Emma Byford (54) - laundress
George Smith (45) - boot maker & post messenger
William Mower (28) - police constable.

About one half of the buildings shown on the 1875 map are still there.

Old windmills in Mill Lane

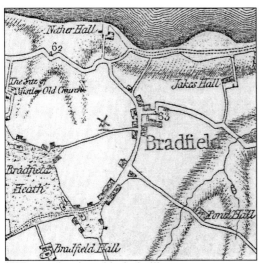

1777 map showing old windmill

Before 1881, to the south west of the church, near Mill Lane, once stood two windmills. Their exact locations are not known and there is conflicting evidence from early maps. This extract from a 1777 map shows one mill to the north side of Mill Lane, but other maps show two on the south side. It may be that the road was rerouted at some time or, perhaps, the mill symbol on the map was just placed roughly in the right area. As the mills are not shown on maps after 1825 it is likely that they were demolished long before 1881.

Map of The Street from Malting House to the Methodist Chapel in Heath Road

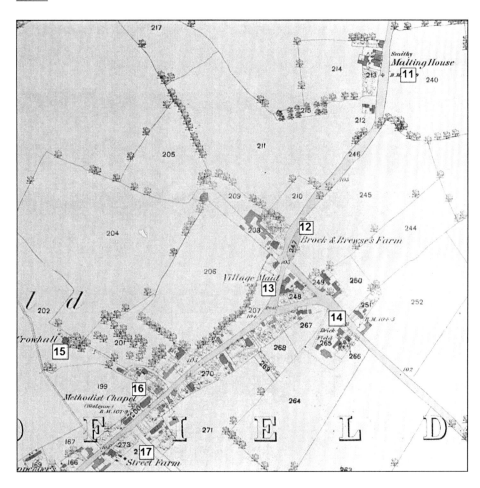

Moving on down The Street we come to Malting House and the village blacksmiths.

Malting House (11 on map)

Ann Wright, a widow (aged 85), was living at the Malting House in 1881. Also living there was her nephew Smith Bawtree (55), a retired farmer. Both were born at Great Oakley and a few years earlier had run a 300 acre farm there. A housekeeper Ann Burgess (54) also lived at the Malting House.

Adjacent was the village blacksmiths. Henry Nunn (56) was the village smith/farrier. He was assisted by George Southgate (31) who lived in Wix Road.

Brock & Brewse's Farm (12 on map)

Brock & Brewse's was a farm of 180 acres and employed six men and three boys. Mulliner J Bullimer (58) farmed here in 1881 and he also ran Malting Farm (see above) and Bartrum/Bartons Farm. He lived here with his wife Mary (58) and their son John (25).

The Village Maid (13 on map)

The Village Maid   (Photo : Nigel Klammer, 2001)

The current Village Maid pub, on the triangular piece of land between Heath Road and Wix Road, was built in the late 1850s replacing an older beer house.

William Felgate was the landlord of the Village Maid in 1881. He was aged 35 and lived with his wife Eleanor (31) and their three children, Eleanor (6), William (4), and Mary (1).

Also resident at the Village Maid was their domestic servant Gertrude Frost (13) and Charles Scott (34), a lodger who was an agricultural labourer.

The Brick Field in Wix Road (14 on map)

Two families associated with brick making were living in Wix Road in 1881.

Francis Puxley (59) was a brickmaster (described elsewhere as a brick, tile and drainpipe maker) employing two men and a boy. His wife was Harriet (60).

Thomas Osgood (47), who was born in Thatcham, Berkshire is listed as a brickmaker and his wife Harriet (47) was a tailoress. They lived with their seven children aged between seven months and 18 years. It is possible that Osgood was Puxley's journeyman.

Crow Hall (15 on map)

Richard Miller (30) an agricultural labourer and his wife Eleanor (32) lived at Crow Hall in 1881, with their five children who were aged between six months and 8 years.

The Wesleyan Methodist Chapel (16 on map)

Bradfield's Methodist church in Heath Road was built about 1850, replacing an earlier chapel that was built in the late 1700s. So far as we can discover, no pictures of the first chapel exist but it has been suggested that the west wall of the current building is made of bricks from the first. The present vestry may also be older than the present church building.

John Wesley's Methodist movement began in 1739 but did not formally break from the established church until 1795. Methodism made a relatively early start in this part of the country and there was a society in Mistley in 1785 that was visited in that year by John Wesley himself. By 1789 worship started in Bradfield. Early members were extremely keen and self-sacrificing in their support of the work and appeared as very generous financial supporters of the Harwich Circuit. In 1813 Bradfield sent £9 to the Quarterly Meeting which was more than Manningtree and Harwich managed to send. This was not a sign of wealth but rather of generosity.

Old postcard of the Methodist Church, c1910

Certainly that first chapel was put to wonderful use and society membership grew fast. In less than 60 years the congregation had outgrown the building. It is said that in the late 1840s the services were packed to the walls and many were unable to get into the building. It was then that the site was cleared and services transferred to a barn whilst the present chapel was built, provided free by the local builder and the remaining labour provided freely by the members.

In 1881 James Lott was the preacher at the church.

For about 100 years the white pinnacle of the Methodist Church was a feature of the village skyline, but time and the weather took their toll on the structure and urgent attention became necessary. In 1994 an exact replica of the original was completed. Church members decided to add a time capsule in the pinnacle for future residents of the village.

Street Farm (17 on map)

William Jennings (51) was the farm bailiff at Street Farm in 1881 where he lived with his wife Sarah (52).

Other houses in Heath Road

At other unidentified houses in Heath Road the household heads included:-

John Cutting (29) - carpenter
Frederick Cutting (23) - bricklayer
Sophie Sargeant (44) - tailoress
Mary Gilbert (38) - tailoress
Sarah Tovell (60) - laundress
John Scott (72) - retired blacksmith.

Other houses in Wix Road

At other unidentified houses in Wix Road lived:-

Elizabeth Mason (44) - tailoress
Isaac Frost (49) - railway labourer
Emily Frost (43) - tailoress
William Greenwood (55) - tailor
George Southgate (31) - blacksmith.

Martha Rowland (43) – tailoress, lived in Dairy House Lane.

Map from the Methodist Chapel to the Primitive Methodist Chapel and down to Barrack Street

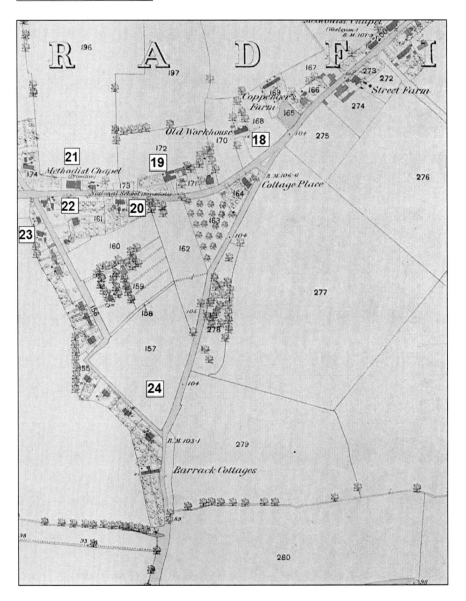

Heath Road from Dairy House Lane

In 1871, about 15 families, mainly employed in farming, were living along this stretch of road. They included an engine driver, two millers and a farm bailiff. James Lott, an agricultural labourer, lived with his wife Mary Ann, a schoolmistress.

By 1881, the residents included a carpenter, butcher, builder, chimney sweep, bricklayer and even a retired actress! She was Sarah Collins, aged 66 and born in Ipswich, boarding in the household of Samuel Adams, an agricultural labourer. No further details of her career have come to light. In 1881, Mary Ann Lott was still a teacher and James was now a gardener and Wesleyan local preacher.

The Old Workhouse (18 on map)

In Medieval times the poor and sick were looked after by the close knit manorial system. After the Black Death and the subsequent break-up of the feudal system the poor mostly relied on the benevolence of the church and monasteries. In the late 1500s, however, after Henry VIII had dissolved the monasteries there was nowhere for the poor to turn. The plight of the poor became so desperate that in 1601 Elizabethan I's Poor Law Act was passed, making the relief of poverty the responsibility of each parish.

Bradfield had its own workhouse in Heath Road. The building held 12 inmates and was in use until 1835. Following an amendment to the Poor Law Act in 1834 villages could no longer be responsible for their own poor and instead parishes were grouped together into a Union that would build a large workhouse to accommodate all the poor from those parishes. As a result, from 1835 the workhouse on Tendring Heath took people from all over the area.

The old workhouse is now a private house called Heath Cottage.

The Ram & Hoggett Inn (19 on map)

The Ram & Hoggett (Photo : Nigel Klammer c1980s)

Run from the 1860s to about 1900 by the Cracknell family, this inn was noted by local people for its sack – a sherry-type drink. After the death of her husband Samuel in 1870, Eliza Cracknell kept the beerhouse and Post Office, and is also described in other censuses as a farmer and pork butcher.

In 1881 she was living here, aged 57, with two sons, Richard (22), a butcher and Frederic (24), a railway clerk. Boarding with them was Fanny Sargeant (20) a pupil teacher, who was probably working at the Bradfield Heath National School a few hundred yards away.

Later proprietors named in street directories included Horatio Nelson Clatworthy, Henry Youngman and Mrs. Cecilia Catchpole.

The Ram & Hoggett closed in the mid-1990s and is now a private house.

The National School (20 on map)

It might seem unusual to have two National Schools, both designated for boys and girls, in a small village. But the series of Education Acts in the late 19th century made basic education compulsory and led to increased demand for school places. The existence of two schools at this time confirms that Bradfield had two separate centres of population, the established village and the heath, and these had not yet been joined up by housing. Both schools were superseded when the current school, located midway between the two in Heath Road, opened in 1907.

Primitive Methodist Chapel (21 on map)

Primitive Methodism is a body of evangelists within the Methodist denomination that developed in the United States and began in England in the early 1800s. A breakaway group from the Wesleyan mainstream, they emphasised simplicity in worship and buildings, concentrated on the rural poor rather than the middle classes and promoted lay ministry. In 1932 the church merged with the Wesleyan

Old postcard showing the Primitive Methodist church (left)

Methodist Church and the United Methodists to form the Methodist Church of Great Britain.

The 1861 census records a Primitive Methodist minister, Benjamin Bell, (born Yarmouth) lodging in Barrack Street with William Abbott, a shoemaker and his wife.

By 1870, the congregation was large enough to need a substantial building and the Bradfield Primitive Methodist Chapel was founded.

The foundation stone was laid at 3pm on Good Friday 15 April 1870, with an address from the Revd. S. Smith. Tea was provided at 5pm and there was a sermon from the Revd. W. Hammond.

At that time the church was part of the Ipswich Circuit and services were held at 2pm and 6pm every Sunday and at 7.30pm on alternate Mondays. The preachers from the circuit were assisted by James Lott who was the preacher at Bradfield's Wesleyan Methodist church.

The chapel was severely damaged by the Great Storm in 1987. The current village shop/post office was built on part of the site in 1957 and a modern bungalow occupies the rest.

The Corner House, Barrack Street (22 on map)

The Chapman & Andre map of 1777 shows a building on this site. Now a private house, it was a shop from the 1890s until the 1950s.

In the 1871 census, Meshach Gould (37) is described as a grocer and dealer living at this address with his wife Eliza (also 37) though it is not clear whether his shop was in this building.

When the 1881 census was taken, Robert Gould (39), an agricultural labourer, was living here with his family, consisting of his wife Emma (39), six children aged between one and 12 years, a married daughter aged 20 and a 12-day old grandchild.

By 1901, George Gammer (48), a grocer's carter, and his wife Hannah (47), described as a grocer and shopkeeper, were in occupation, with daughter Emily.

They were followed by the King family, and by Gordon Sparkes and family in 1934.

This corner of Heath Road and Barrack Street has been known by the name of several local families - Lotts Corner (1861), Kings Corner, and more recently, as Sparkes Corner.

View Windmill Road from Barrack Street in about 1920

North View, Barrack Street (23 on map)

This house and its associated outbuildings were a butcher's shop and slaughterhouse. George Watts Syrett and his wife Caroline ran it from the 1860s to his death in 1894, followed by his son Frederick.

In 1881 he is shown aged 62, a butcher employing one man and living with his wife Caroline, aged 60. Their two daughters, Hannah (28), a dressmaker, and Sarah (22), a servant, were living with them.

Walter Partridge took over in the 1930s when Mr. Sparkes bought the corner shop.

Barrack Street in 1881 had a number of small cottages mainly inhabited by agricultural labourers. Interspersed were patches of open ground, the remains of the old heath or common land, now fast disappearing under allotments and gardens.

Probable site of the Napoleonic barracks (24 on map)

It has been suggested that two regiments of East and West Essex militia were encamped on Bradfield Heath in 1803 and possibly later to respond to threats of invasion.

A marginal note in the Bradfield burials register confirms this and several baptisms, marriages and burials for the militia are recorded for 1803, indicating that many of the soldiers were accompanied by their families. Most of the burials were of babies, suggesting perhaps that living conditions were primitive in what was almost certainly an encampment under canvas.

The exact location has not been recorded, but local memory suggests it may have been this field as it appears to have been levelled off to form a plateau. It has also been suggested that some of the cottages dotted around may have been built as officers' quarters, though they do not have a particularly military appearance. Ellis Road (formerly Stephenson Lane) makes an impressive dogleg around something no longer there, possibly the camp entrance with guard post.

Others living in Cansey Lane

In 1871 some eight or nine families were living here (possibly in cottages belonging to Golden Ferry Farm). Almost all were agricultural labourers, born in Bradfield or close by. It was a similar picture in 1881 but the surnames are different, suggesting that farm workers were a mobile group at this time. Others living in Cansey Lane in 1881, who were not agricultural labourers, were:

William Hammond (65) – gardener
Walter Manning (38) – general dealer.

Map of Bradfield Hall and Steam Mill

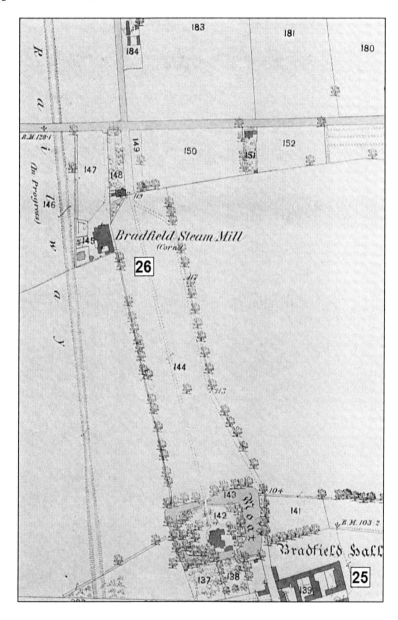

Bradfield Hall (25 on map)

Bradfield Hall

Bradfield Hall was built by Sir John Rainsford about 1520 and was later the home of the Grimston family. Surrounded by a moat, the brick building comprised two storeys plus attics.

At the time of its demolition in 1955 it was a rectangular block with a semi-octagonal stair turret at the S.W. angle. Inside the building were some 17th century doors and panelling, and a spiral oak staircase running to the top of the house round a central wooden pier said to have been a single tree. The rails at the top had symmetrically turned balusters dating from around 1600. There was a private chapel adjoining the hall in which marriages and funerals were solemnised. A new house was erected on the same moated site as the old Hall.

John H Green (54) farmed the 365 acres at Bradfield Hall in 1881 and employed 12 men and 5 boys. He lived with his wife Sarah (53) and their two sons Harcourt (20) and Frederick (18). Also in the household were Robert Robinson (34), farm servant and his wife Ellen (30), domestic servant/cook and Eliza Clements (16), housemaid.

Bradfield Steam Mill (26 on map)

Bradfield's steam mill was originally a windmill and probably built around 1840. In 1857 Patrick Daniels bought it and he quickly set about installing steam power. Apparently, he put the mill to use day and night and only a few months after the mill's conversion the machinery overheated and it caught fire, destroying most of the building and large quantities of corn and flour. The damage to the building was restored at an estimated cost of £2,000.

In 1881 Harry Daniels (29) was miller and corn merchant employing six men. Maria Bull (52) was his housekeeper.

With the advent of 20th century technology and economics, many mills became defunct, and the steam mill was no exception. Had the proposed Mistley, Thorpe and Walton Railway materialised, the mill (which was built alongside the route, probably with potential transport prospects in mind) might have lasted longer.

During the 20th century the old mill was put to various uses, but in 1989 the building again caught fire causing much damage.

Map along Windmill Road and King Street

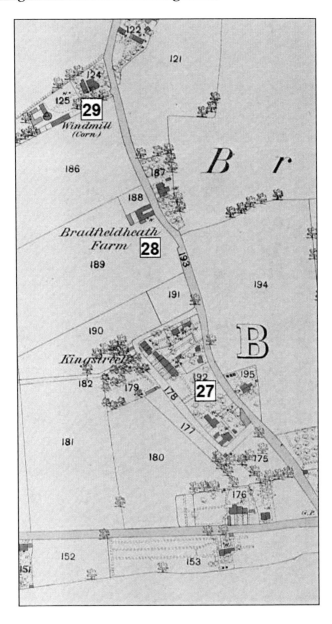

Cherry Tree (Beer house) (27 on map)

James Byford (33) was butcher and beer house keeper. He lived at the Cherry Tree with his wife Alice (27) and their four children. Also living there were two agricultural labourers – Arthur Prior (19) and James Lungley (28).

Bradfield Heath Farm (28 on map)

Mary Ann Sparrow (63) lived at the farm and Catherine Newman (24), boarder - National School Mistress.

Tower Mill (29 on map)

This tower mill was built about 1844, on the west side of Windmill Road, south of the junction with Mill Lane and behind "The Nook". The first miller was Robert Birch Brown.

In 1881 Bernard Sparrow (47) was miller and farmer of 14 acres and employed one man. He lived with his wife Mary (41) and at the time the census was taken Bernard's sister Anne (50) was visiting.

On 20 December 1911, a severe storm hit Bradfield which broke the sails of the mill and did much damage to the roof and mill's mechanism. It appears that the mill's sails were removed and the other damage repaired as the mill continued to work for some years powered by an oil engine. It was demolished in 1934.

Tower Mill

Other houses in King Street

Other residents of King Street or nearby included (in addition to several agricultural workers):-

Charles Crick (48) - bricklayer and mole catcher and his son Caleb, a bricklayer's labourer
Ann Collins (64) – laundress
Jasper Porter (61) - chimney sweep
Ann Partridge (56) - nurse
Abram Gosling (56) - thatcher and gardener.

Map of Windmill Road from Dove House Farm to Slipes Farm

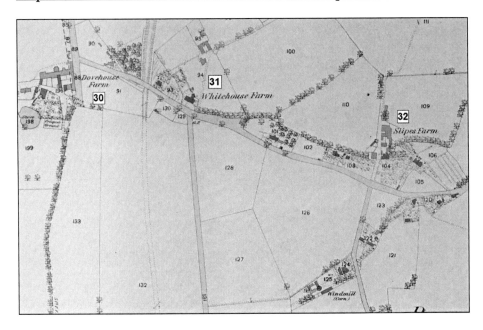

Dove House Farm (30 on map)

Samuel Felgate (42) was farmer and bailiff of 369 acres employing 11 men and two boys. He lived with his wife Eliza (54) and son Samuel (14).

White House (31 on map)

In 1881 Mrs Elizabeth Budd, aged 70, lived here with her daughter Jeanette Budd (35) and their servant Matilda Robinson (22).

Slipes Farm (32 on map)

Henry Kerridge (64) farmed 100 acres here, with his wife Mary (33) and their four children.

Map from Nether Hall to Stour Lodge

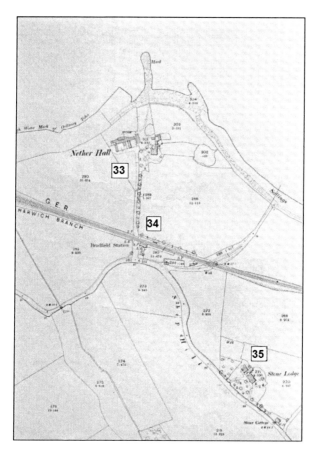

Nether Hall (33 on map)

Nether Hall   (Photo : Nigel Klammer)

Nether Hall is of Georgian origin although it has been modified and altered over the years. In the late 1700s it was owned by the Rigby family who farmed 227 acres along the shore. Most of this land has over the years been sold off to other farmers.

For centuries a causeway had run from Manningtree to Wrabness along the foreshore and was used by horses and carriages to avoid the many steep hills inland from the estuary. Most traffic therefore passed Nether Hall on its way to and from Manningtree and Harwich. There was also a landing stage ("hard") for barges which until the early 20th century was used to send such produce as straw to the London markets and to receive in return horse manure for fertilizer for the fields.

In 1881 James Ferris (68) lived here with his wife Emma (64), daughter Emma (38) and granddaughter Eva May (10). They had a servant Sarah Ann Gooch (19). The farm covered 270 acres and they employed seven labourers.

Railway Station (34 on map)

James Harrison (65) was the stationmaster and lived in the station house with his wife Sarah (56), daughter Ruth (19), a general servant and son Arthur (16) who was a station porter.

Stour Lodge (35 on map)

Stour Lodge   (Photo : Nigel Klammer)

Stour Lodge was built in the Regency period in 1823. Its owners included Lewis Agassiz who served with the 3rd Battalion of the Royal Marines during the Anglo-American War in 1814-15. He died in 1866, aged 73. There is a memorial to him in St Lawrence Church.

Mr R Bolton Barton (61) who was a magistrate and barrister-at-law lived at Stour Lodge in 1881. He and his wife Eliza Ann (55) had spent some time in the East Indies where their daughter Eliza (18) was born. His sister-in-law Jessie Dalton (43) stayed with them. There were three servants: Sarah Bradbrook (31) cook, Susanne Farrow (30), housemaid and Emma Watts (20), under housemaid.

Map of Jacques Hall and Ragmarsh Farm

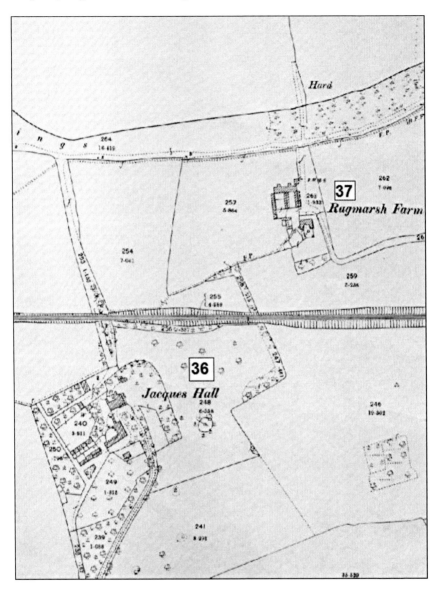

Between Stour Lodge and Jacques Hall was Rose Cottage (now Bradfield End) and in 1881 the head of the household was John Robertson. He was 82 years old, so was actually born in the previous century – 1799. He lived there with his niece Julia Lees (40) who was a chemist's wife and their servant Ellen Jennings (23). Also visiting them at the time was Clara Alexander (18).

Jacques Hall (36 on map)

Jacques Hall   (Photo : Nigel Klammer c1987)

It is believed that the hamlet of Bradfield Manston mentioned in the Domesday book was sited at or near what is now Jacques Hall. After the Norman Conquest, Bradfield Manston was given to Roger de Ramis.

During the reign of Henry II, William de Ramis conveyed it to Aubrey de Vere, Earl of Oxford, to hold as a quarter of a knight's fee. Part belonged to Ralph Fitz-Adam, and later Philip de St Osith who passed it on to John de Kirkby who leased it to Robert, Earl of Oxford, thereby "paying to the chief lords all due services and to himself clove gilly-flower". It was held by various partnerships under the 7th and 8th Earls of Oxford and in 1568 William Cardinal rented it for 3s 4d per year.

As we have seen earlier Jacques Hall derived its name from the son of Sir John Rainsford in about 1540.

At the beginning of the last century it was the home of the Dunning family, and its last private owner was Captain Rolfe.

In 1964 it became a Spastics Society Home for the next 22 years, and in 1988 became a Therapeutic Centre for teenage victims of crime and assault.

Restored in the early 1880s in the Jacobean style, the present house was built beside the site of a sub-nunnery to Wix, the chapel of which was dedicated to the Virgin Mary and known as "Our Lady in the Oats".

In 1881 Jacques Hall was owned by George Simpson Hardy. The Hardy family had owned the Hall for many years. George Hardy does not appear in the 1881 census for Bradfield. He also owned Ramsey Hall, just a few miles away, and he appears in that village's census where he is recorded along with his wife Mary (31) and their son George Douglas (7). There were several people living at Jacques Hall at that time including:-

James Tovell (55) - farmer's bailiff and his son James (23) - groom
Thomas Balls (40) - groom and gardener
James Totham (32) - coachman and groom.

Ragmarsh Farm (37 on map)

On July 20, 1571 William Littlebury of Dedham made his will. In it he made provision for a yearly stipend from his farm at Ragmarsh to pay for a schoolmaster to be installed at the existing schoolroom and adjoining master's house in Dedham. He stipulated that the master should be a university graduate and should teach, free, 20 children from the poorest families in Dedham, Ardleigh, Great Bromley, Stratford and Bradfield.

The school was incorporated by letters of patent on May 14, 1575 and named "The Free Grammar School of Queen Elizabeth in Dedham". The 23 trustees of Littlebury's will and the vicar of Dedham were appointed as the school governors with power to take £40 per year from Ragmarsh and other property.

John W Green farmed 174 acres here in 1881 and employed 6 men and 2 boys. Emma Chivers (38) was a general servant. Two of the labourers Robert Childs (58) and Harry Finch (17) were staying in the farmhouse at the time of the census.

Other houses in Harwich Road

Amongst the other people living in the houses in Harwich Road were:-

Richard Edwards (60) - grocer and draper
George Gildes (28) - chemist
George Finch (48) - railway platelayer.

This takes our tour full circle, back to St Lawrence Church where we started.

We have seen that in the 1880s Bradfield was a thriving rural, agricultural village that was largely self-sufficient. It had several shops, pubs and churches and village life and comradeship would have been at the heart of everyone's existence. We will see in the following chapters that many changes occurred over the following century that have gradually turned Bradfield into the village we now know.

Chapter 6

Into the 20th century

> Some key historical dates:-
>
> - 1901   Edward VII
> - 1910   George V
> - 1914-1918   First World War

In the remaining chapters of this book the authors have described what they think are some of the more important or interesting aspects of life in Bradfield over the last century or so. It is by no means a complete story of events, but hopefully gives the reader a feel for how village life has changed over the passage of time.

A Shaky Start

In 1884, just three years after our "tour" around Bradfield, an event occurred that literally would have shaken villagers. On 22 April at 9.18am the UK's most destructive earthquake for more than 400 years struck near Colchester. The epicentre was a few miles south of Colchester and, lasting for around 20 seconds, the quake measured 4.6 on the Richter scale. The effects were not only felt across England but also across northern France and Belgium.

The quake resulted in only a handful of deaths, but caused many injuries and much structural damage to towns and villages in north east Essex. No doubt the shock waves would have been felt in Bradfield and must have been a very frightening experience for everyone.

Water Supply

Until the late 19th century, rainwater was the only source of water in Bradfield and surrounding areas. Even in the local towns rainwater had to be stored in tanks or water collected from wells for washing and cleaning. At that time it is likely that Bradfield's drinking water would have been brought in from Mistley.

Many of the village's cottages and houses would have had wells in their back gardens, which would have been shared with close neighbours who would have been granted access. This tradition would have existed from time immemorial and, even in the 1850s, the thought of a clean healthy supply of water to all houses was just a distant dream.

In 1853 Peter Bruff, a civil engineer, was commissioned by Harwich Corporation to find a reliable supply of water and to pipe this to local towns and villages. This task was not an easy one and it was not until the late 1880s that this was fully achieved. Harwich received its first supply in 1887 via the first main laid by Tendring Hundred Waterworks Co.

In 1888 mains were laid from Wix Cross through Thorpe and Upper Kirby to Frinton, and in May 1889, the supply from Frinton to Walton was finally connected.

So, whilst it took him a very long time, the village folk of Bradfield and surrounding villages should have been eternally grateful to Peter Bruff for his unending efforts to bring a good clean piped water supply to the village.

The Bicycle

In the late 19th century moving around the village would have been quite slow. You might have ridden a horse, or perhaps a "penny farthing" or, if you were well off, perhaps a pony and trap. Failing that you would have had to walk. All this was to change in the 1890s. The "safety" bicycle was invented in around 1880. It had a great advantage over the "penny farthing" with its huge wheel which made balancing and steering difficult. The chain driven "safety" with two smaller wheels and pneumatic tyres proved immediately popular and, within the next ten years, had become a common means of transport.

The bicycle became a passport to the freedom of the countryside and, with the advantages of mass production, gradually became within the means of ordinary workers and their families. Not only was it used for recreational purposes, but also for trade, with bicycles fitted with front carriers enabling goods to be delivered more quickly across the village.

Here is evidence that Bradfield was not slow to follow the bicycle craze. The photo shows five riders with their mounts outside the cottage on the corner of Harwich Road (now Milestones) in about 1905.

Photo of the cottage on the corner of Harwich Road (opposite the Plough) in about 1905

A New Pub

In about 1906 the present Strangers Home was built on the site of an earlier public house, The White Horse, at the junction of Harwich Road and The Street. Little is known about The White Horse except that it was a single storey building, and some of its walls are thought to remain inside the construction of the Strangers Home.

The first landlord of the new Strangers Home was Mr J Clarke who remained until 1933.

The new Strangers Home with Model T Ford Van (Reg. HJ 309) in about 1930

Education

The Education Act of 1891 introduced free schooling, where fees up to 10 shillings per week (50p) would be paid by the state. As a result, there was a greater demand for schooling and by the early 1900s Bradfield's small schools were unable to keep up with the demand for places. So a new, larger school was built to accommodate more children.

The "new Council School" (now Bradfield Primary School) in Heath Road opened on 7 January 1907 with 128 pupils. The first headmaster was Mr. J. W. Bolton and his wife was the infant teacher. Their daughters also taught, along with Miss Fisher and Miss Chatworthy.

Mr. Bolton died on 15 March 1918, and his wife remained temporarily in charge until the appointment of Mr. Ernest Jones, who took over as head on 1 July 1918.

Mr. Jones remained until 29 September 1950. During these years the number of pupils steadily declined from 138 to 86, as fewer families found local farm employment. The war years showed a dramatic reduction in the number of

79

pupils, as the older children were needed to help on the farms while the men were at war. In 1945 the school registered only 76 pupils, but by 1948 the number had recovered to 101.

The new "Council School" shortly after it opened in 1907

Cars and Buses

It was about 1905 that the first two motor cars could be seen driving around the village. One belonged to Sir Edwin Dunning of Jacques Hall and the other to Allen Large who ran the local general store. Over the next decade or two, as the number of motorised vehicles increased, Mr Large expanded his business and came to own lorries, cars and a bus.

The red Daimler bus was a state of the art affair in its time, top speed of 12 mph, cruising at 10 mph when potholes and the solid tyres on cast iron wheels permitted. It had hard seats inside and an open area for freight, a tailboard for bulky items and crates of chickens for the Saturday Colchester market. It was a carrier's vehicle designed for the people of the village to travel to Ipswich and Colchester, spend three hours or so in the town and return laden with their shopping. Constant stops for people to board and alight, and for parcels to be delivered, meant that the journey took up to four hours each way. It is thought that the bus probably started its rounds just before the First World War and continued until 1924. In 1925 the Daimler had been replaced by a Model T Ford Van as it was decided to concentrate on freight, leaving the passenger trade to firms such as Beeston and Hooks. The Model T was less cumbersome, easier to drive, had balloon tyres and was faster until you came to a hill when you stopped and selected the only other gear – low – very low. The Ford would reach 20 mph.

In the early days of the 20th century, if you wanted to go to town, other than by train, you would have travelled by horse driven carrier's cart, courtesy of Large Stores from 1908 starting at Acacia House (opposite the Stranger's Home) and then later by their red motor bus.

Possibly the first proper motor bus service to work locally in the Tendring Hundred was the Clacton and District Motor Service Company, which was registered on 4 December 1913 and during the first war owned about three vehicles. Another early carrier was Hook Brothers of Wix.

A Hook Brothers (Wix) onmibus

With so many local pioneer public transport providers about, the inevitable happened and the smaller ones were swallowed up by bigger companies. By the

1920s many firms were merged, much like the railway companies in the mid-19th century.

Scouting

The scouting movement began in 1907 through the efforts of Robert Baden-Powell. The stated aim of The Scout Association is to "promote the development of young people in achieving their full physical, intellectual, social and spiritual potential, as individuals, as responsible citizens and as members of their local, national and international communities". The scouting movement spread very quickly in the UK and the parish magazine of June 1910 records that on 18 May a meeting took place in Bradfield at which 18 boys joined under the stewardship of Mr Brunning the scoutmaster. According to the troop's records, however, it was not formally registered until September 1914. This Bradfield troop continues to this day.

Church Lych Gate

The Church Lych Gate

In 1911 a lych gate was built at the entrance to St Lawrence Church.

On Whit Monday evening in 1911, the gate, which was erected by the parishioners of Bradfield to commemorate the 27 years incumbency of the Revd. C J Newman (from 1883 to 1910), was dedicated by the Revd. T K Norman in the presence of a large congregation of parishioners. The gate was designed and built by Mr W Polley of Coggeshall.

Coronation of King George V

On 22 June 1911 villagers celebrated the Coronation of King George V. The following is an extract from the Mistley-cum-Bradfield Parish Magazine:-

"On 22 June, Coronation Day arrived at last. Throughout the country towns and villages were gay with bunting. Bradfield was one among the many villages that recognised it as a great and important day. The morning broke grey and dull and the sky continued overcast throughout the day, but fortunately no rain fell. At half-past one there was a service in the Parish Church, which was largely attended. At 3 o'clock, sports were held in the Rectory Meadow, in which young and old joined with much pleasure. An excellent meat tea was provided which everyone did ample justice. Sports of various kinds were indulged in till 9.15, when the prizes were distributed by Mrs WB Nichols and Mrs TK Norman. At 9.30, the fireworks were lighted, many of which shot into the sky and lighted the dark fields for a few moments, then breaking into many stars fell to the ground. With a hearty singing of "God Save the King" the party broke up, and so ended the memorable and happy day at Bradfield".

The Bradfield Coal & Clothing Club

During the late 1800s Bradfield's Coal and Clothing Club was established. The Club's purpose was to help villagers save for Christmas when pay-outs would have been made. There were strict rules to ensure that the Club helped the poorer people in the village and may have been set up under the initiative of the church.

By August 1911, according to the parish magazine, the Club seems to have fallen into some financial difficulties, with Canon

BRADFIELD COAL AND CLOTHING CLUBS.						
	£	s.	d.	£	s.	d.
Deposits by Members	66	7	4			
Subscriptions—						
Miss Barlow	12	6				
Mr. Gammer	11	6				
Mr. E. O. Green	10	8				
Mr. Stone	15	9				
Mr. Catling	1	10	4			
Donation—						
Canon Norman & Rev. T. K. Norman, to balance	10	6	0			
Mr. Gammer for Coal				11	0	2
Mr. E. O. Green, ditto				10	5	0
Mr. Stone, ditto				14	8	11
Mr. Catling, ditto				28	15	0
Mr. Gammer for Clothing				5	4	2
Mr. Joyce				5	17	10
Mr. Mead				3	17	6
Mr. Parsons				15	6	
	£80	14	1	£80	14	1

Norman and the Revd. Norman having to make donations to cover the balance of the liabilities for that year. As a result a change to the rules was implemented so that "no members earning more than £1 per week can be accepted", presumably in an attempt to reduce the Club's liabilities.

Sporting Activities

Sporting activities have, no doubt, always been part of village life. There were, of course, local football and cricket teams, but there was also great competitiveness in a lesser known sport of the day. During the first part of the last century, and perhaps before that, there were quoit league and cup competitions between local villages. At that time Bradfield Street and Bradfield Heath were seen as two distinct villages and there appears to have been strong rivalry between the two when it came to the serious business of quoits.

To many people the game of quoits will probably conjure up memories of a game played with rope hoops and wooden pegs (deck quoits). The quoits played seriously in Bradfield and district was very different to this. Traditional quoits is a game played with metal hoops, usually made of steel, and thrown across a set distance at a metal spike (called a pin, hob or mott). The spike is centrally, and vertically, positioned in a square of moist clay measuring three feet across. There were three versions of the game in England – the "northern" game, the "long" game and the "East Anglian" game. It was probably the last of these that was played in Bradfield.

The competition locally was for teams of six with the winning team being the first to reach 60 points. The Mistley-cum-Bradfield Parish Magazine for July 1911 lists the following results of two league matches between Bradfield Street and Bradfield Heath. The matches took place on the Rectory lawn.

BRADFIELD STREET versus BRADFIELD HEATH.			
C. Hunebell	12	F. Mason	9
J. Simons	10	F. Gilbert	14
A. Goss	17	A. Chaplin	5
M. Mason	13	J. Southgate	1
F. Gould	6	J. Roberts	10
W. Fox	4	W. Clarke	7
Total	62	Total	46

BRADFIELD STREET *versus* BRADFIELD HEATH.			
E. Simons........	8	T. Mason........	7
C. Hunebell......	6	F. Gilbert	9
J. Simons........	6	J. Southgate	7
Jim Simons	18	A. Chaplin	3
A. Goss..........	11	W. Clarke	3
M. Mason........	13	J. Roberts	3
Total....	62	Total......	32

It would seem that in 1911 Bradfield Street had the edge. Perhaps at some time in the future Bradfield Heath might challenge Bradfield Street to a rematch!

First World War

Over the decade or so before the outbreak of the First World War there was much political uncertainty across Europe. The threat of a European war must have been felt throughout the country. In the early 1900s an arms race developed. Envious of Britain's superior navy Germany, France and Russia substantially strengthened their military might.

Concerned about Britain's defences in the event of war, the Territorial Army was created in 1908 made up of volunteers. Territorials normally have a full-time job or career and their civilian jobs are protected, to some extent, should they be compulsorily mobilised. As the name suggests, the Territorial Army's original purpose was home defence and the force was under no obligation to serve overseas. However, after the outbreak of war in August 1914, Territorial units were given the option of serving in France and before the end of that month 70 TA battalions had volunteered.

Bradfield was not slow to recruit TA volunteers. On 23 February 1909, a meeting took place in the village and 15 men were recruited on the night. Each recruit received half a sovereign (50p). In today's money 50p is worth about £40, but the actual half sovereign gold coin would today be worth more than twice that amount.

In 1916 a Zeppelin airship dropped three bombs on Bradfield. These landed in a field at the far end of Cansey Lane past Golden Ferry farm. It is thought that the

Zeppelin was not directly attacking Bradfield but had taken fright and jettisoned part of its deadly cargo with a view to hightailing home.

During the period of the war from 1914 to 1918 a total of 156 Bradfield men served in the armed forces and fought for their country. Most served in the army for many different regiments, but some saw service with the naval and flying services. As everyone knows, the loss of human life in the First World War was very high and of the 156 serving Bradfield men 21 died in action or from their wounds.

Bradfield's most famous war time hero was Squadron Commander Edwin Harris Dunning of Jacques Hall. On 2 August 1917 be became the first pilot to land a plane successfully on the deck of a moving ship.

Commander Dunning landing his plane on HMS Furious in 1917

Commander Dunning was born in 1892, and was awarded the DSC for gallantry during the First World War while serving on HMS Furious. He made two successful landings, but was unfortunately killed on his third attempt five days later.

According to a letter to his father from the Admiralty, "the data obtained was of the utmost value. It will make airplanes indispensable to a fleet and possibly revolutionise naval warfare".

Dunning's bravery is commemorated on a memorial in St Lawrence Church.

On 4 August 1918 a special service was held in St Lawrence Church on the fourth anniversary of the outbreak of war. The collection at the service raised £7:1s:0¼d (that's nearly £300 in today's terms) for prisoners of war.

After the war, on 24 August 1919, a special service was held in St Lawrence Church to dedicate the memorials to those who died and served in the war. One, a memorial tablet in the church (from parishioners), was to those who died, and another was the war memorial column in the churchyard (from the Dunning family) which lists all those who served.

The church was packed and many failed to get in for the service. The band of the 1st Cheshires headed a procession of servicemen down The Street and then accompanied most of the musical part of the service which was concluded by the Dead March and the Last Post. The Petition to Dedicate was read by Sir Edwin Dunning (Squadron Commander Dunning's father).

The memorial tablet fund raised more than £172 (over £6,000 in today's terms). Of that amount nearly £100 (£3,600 today) was raised by parishioners and Miss Pattrick's jumble sale raised over £51 (more than £1,800 today). The following gives details of the memorial tablet fund that parishioners subscribed to:-

———— MEMORIAL TABLET FUND. ————
Balance Sheet.

Receipts.	£	s.	d.	Expenditure.	£	s.	d.	£	s.	d.
Whist Drive, per Mrs. Large	11	0	6	James Powell & Sons, Memorial Tablet	145	0	0			
Concert, per Mrs. Large and Mrs. Clatworthy	7	3	3	Carriage and Fixing	10	0	0			
Organ Recital, per Mr. Moakson	3	8	4½	Memorial Brass	4	15	0			
Jumble Sale, per Miss Pattrick	51	8	9	Fixing	10	0				
Subscriptions	99	17	11	Faculty	1	1	6			
								161	6	6
				Wiles & Son, Balance Sheet, Block, &c.	4	6	6			
				Balance	7	5	9½			
	£172	18	9½					£172	18	9½

A FORM OF SERVICE

Used at the Church of St. Lawrence,

BRADFIELD,

On the Feast of St. Bartholomew,

SUNDAY, AUGUST 24th, 1919,

WHEN THE

Memorial Column

ERECTED TO THE MEMORY OF THE MEN OF BRADFIELD
WHO HAVE SERVED THEIR COUNTRY IN THE GREAT WAR

WAS DEDICATED,

AND THE

Addition to the Churchyard

Kindly presented to the Parish by Sir Edwin Dunning,

WAS CONSECRATED

BY THE

Right Rev. the LORD BISHOP OF COLCHESTER,

AT WHICH SERVICE THE

Stained Glass Windows and Memorial Tablets

ERECTED TO THE MEMORY OF

SQUADRON COMMANDER EDWIN HARRIS DUNNING,
AND D.S.C., R.N.,

LIEUTENANT ALSELAN BUCHANAN NICHOLS,

IST ESSEX REGT.,

WERE ALSO DEDICATED.

The War Memorial in St Lawrence Churchyard

88

Chapter 7

Between the Wars and beyond

Some key historical dates:-

- 1936   Edward VIII
- 1936   George VI
- 1939-1945   Second World War
- 1952   Elizabeth II

There is only one shop in Bradfield today, but this, of course, has not always been the case. As we have already seen, from our 1881 tour of the village, there were various shops and traders serving the village community. This was true for much of the 20th century.

Mr G Sparkes came to Bradfield in 1922 and purchased an existing general store in The Street. This was close to the general store run by Allen Large & Sons (now Acacia House) where there was also a small garage with petrol pumps. Mr Large also ran a carrier service in his light van and single-decker bus. In 1934, Mr Sparkes purchased the shop at Kings Corner (now Sparkes Corner). The butchers associated with this business was taken over by the Partridge family, whose shop and slaughterhouse adjoined North House in Barrack Street.

In addition to the main village stores there were also small sweet shops and villagers could enjoy the treat of an ice-cream from a man who came from Dedham. Opposite the Village Maid was a hut where fresh fish was sold.

In 1957 Mr Sparkes acquired the site adjacent to the Primitive Methodist Church and built the present village shop. In 1967 the village Post Office moved to Mr Sparkes's shop from The Street end of the village.

Electricity, Telephone and Radio

Today we take the power, heat and light that electricity provides for granted. It is hard for us to imagine how we would get on without it. On the rare occasions when there is a power cut, even for a short time, our lives seem to grind to a halt. Whilst industry and some large houses would have had electricity supplied by their own generators in the late 19th century, it was not until the early 20th century that the problems of distributing electricity had been overcome and the slow process of supply to the whole country began. The original demand for more electricity was mainly for street lighting and then to private houses in towns and cities. There were real problems in distributing supply to rural areas and it was not until the early 1930s that electricity came to Bradfield. Until then villagers' houses would have been lit by oil lamps and candles.

Another invention that we nowadays take so much for granted is the telephone. Again, like the supply of electricity, it was the towns and cities that benefited first and gradually the trunk system made it out to rural areas. Amongst the first telephones in Bradfield were those at Stour Lodge, the Post Office and Large's garage.

In 1922 the British Broadcasting Corporation was set up and its first radio programme was transmitted on 14 November that year. Even though this was a full decade or more before Bradfield had electrical power, it is probable that some villagers would have tuned in on "crystal sets" to listen to this wonderful new invention. A crystal set does not need a battery or electricity - it requires no source of power for its operation other than the radio signal itself.

The wireless quickly became a social and cultural phenomenon and King George V learned to use the new medium to address his people. On 23 April 1924 he broadcast for the first time when millions heard his voice as he opened the Wembley Empire exhibition.

It was not until the mid to late 1950s that television became a reality for many people. Although the BBC's television service started in 1934 the service was suspended throughout the Second World War. The cost of television sets was way beyond the means of most people until the 1960s.

Another Railway Accident

On 28 April 1931 there was a train derailment near Bradfield station when trucks, each containing several tons of coal, came off the lines. The railway company righted the trucks with the help of a crane and re-loaded the coal, but not all of the coal was retrieved. Local sheds were filled that winter for the price of a 10 shilling note.

"The Broad Field" – A Pageant

The Pageant programme

In 1932, the Revd. Denis Bayley wrote a Pageant that was performed by many villagers, young and old, at Stour Lodge on 13, 14 and 16 July.

"The Broad Field" consisted of four Acts, each forming a short play of imagined scenes from Bradfield's past in 1155, 1306 and 1644 and the then present day in 1932. A number of the characters in the Pageant were based on some of the real life people from Bradfield's past, including William de Ramis, Sir John de Brokesburne, Sir Harbottle Grimston, and Matthew Hopkins. The proceeds of the Pageant were in aid of the Scout Hut Fund.

More than 150 villagers took part in the pageant, either as performers or in support with its organisation.

Scout Hut

In the mid-1930s a wooden scout hut was built in Harwich Road opposite St Lawrence Church, which soon became a much used meeting place for not just the scouts but also all sorts of village groups.

It was sold in 1960 for £350 and was thereafter used primarily as a church hall.

For many years nearly every Saturday there was a dance, with local bands providing music. The hut was often full, with people enjoying themselves, bouncing on the sprung wooden floor to the beat of the music.

Over the years the building deteriorated and by the mid-1990s it became unsafe. The hall was finally demolished in the early 2000s, but it is good to know that much of the proceeds from the sale of the land on which it stood was put towards the cost of building the new church room extension in 2008.

The old Scout Hut/Church Hall   (photo: Nigel Klammer c1989)

Coronation of King George VI

The four parishes of Lawford, Manningtree, Mistley and Bradfield got together for a celebration on 12 May 1937 of the coronation of King George VI. The event started with a procession from each parish finishing at the park meadow in Mistley. In this photo the lorry (CPU 559) is believed to be Sparkes' lorry which was used for their coal business. Also in the picture is a clown with a decorated bike. This bike when rode looked funny as the seat went up and down giving onlookers great amusement!

Bradfield's parade for King George VI's coronation

Fire Station

Bradfield once had its own Fire Station. It opened in a Nissen hut in Barrack Street in 1938. The alarm bell was on the side wall of the Post Office. The bell rang at night and the bell and siren were used during the day. The men carried on their daily work and came as soon as the alarm went out.

There were 14 retained firemen who were on call in the village and they would deal with on average of about 16 calls a year. The Bradfield pump engine also went to the aid of other villages when necessary.

After some time, Essex County Council took over the service, the owner of the land on which the Fire Station stood died, and the executors winding up the estate asked for the Station to be removed. The cost of buying another piece of land and building another Fire Station would have been about £2,000. With improved equipment at Harwich, Colchester and Manningtree, it was felt that the Station at Bradfield was no longer necessary, being only three miles from Manningtree, seven from Harwich and 11 miles from Colchester. The pump was overhauled and re-issued to another part of the county.

Women's Institute

The Bradfield Afternoon Women's Institute held its first meeting in the Wesleyan Chapel schoolroom in November 1938 and played an important part in village life for more than 47 years. The decision to close the Institute was taken at the A.G.M. in 1985 as, owing to dwindling membership and the increasing age of members, it was impossible to find anyone willing to take office.

Although the Bradfield's Afternoon W.I. no longer exists its Evening W.I., which started in 1969, still prospers.

Second World War

Just like a generation earlier, villagers in the mid-1930s would have been extremely anxious and concerned about the prospect of another war. The country's worst fears were realised when war was declared on 1 September 1939.

Many villagers served in the armed forces during the Second World War. There is a memorial in the church to the five villagers who were killed in action during the conflict.

Perhaps it was during the war that the Women's Institute made its greatest effort. Purchasing fruit from villagers and provided with a special allocation of sugar, members made an amazing 3,111 pounds of jam in 1941/42 which was sent to a centre for distribution to shops for sale on the jam ration. Women worked most afternoons and evenings according to how much fruit there was, making the jam on four oil-stoves in the Wesleyan Chapel schoolroom. Food was not the only shortage that had to be coped with. One evening a lot of fruit had come in when the siren sounded and lights had to be put out as the windows were not blacked out. The sugar had been added and the jam just coming up to the boil so the pans were put into a member's car and rushed to her home for the final cooking.

During the Second World War a number of bombing decoys were built with the aim of misleading the Luftwaffe. Decoys were designed specifically for the protection of naval bases and one such decoy was built near Bradfield in a field along the side of the Stour. The aim of the decoy was to replicate the night-time fires from successful air raids on a specific target. If this worked, it would fool the enemy into thinking that the fire decoy near Bradfield was their target, thereby encouraging them to drop more bombs in that area rather than on

Harwich. Located some distance from the decoy area, the electrical ignition for the fires was controlled from an earth-covered night shelter which housed the generator and switch gear. Although a good idea in theory, it is doubtful if the decoys ever achieved much. It is likely that the fires were not large enough and therefore too dim to be obvious to the enemy's pilots.

Some children were evacuated to Bradfield during the war. They left their homes in east London to come and live with families in the village.

Some American forces were billeted in Bradfield during the war and often took children for rides in their jeeps!

Crosses in bluebell wood in the memory of Mervyn Herbert and Albert Eastwood

Towards the latter part of the war, on 23 March 1943, a very tragic accident occurred in the bluebell wood in Mill Lane. A flying ace Mervyn Horatio Herbert was returning in his Mosquito from a reconnaissance flight over the North Sea in order to link up with an English bomber testing a new radar detection device. It appears that, as he was flying along the Stour, he unfortunately came under friendly fire from an anti-aircraft gunner who was placed on Mistley Quay. The aircraft exploded in mid-air and the main part of the fuselage fell into the bluebell wood. Both Herbert and his navigator, Albert Eastwood were killed.

Mervyn Herbert was the 17th Baron D'arcy de Knayth, and was the great grandson of Baron Robert Clive ("Clive of India").

If you visit the bluebell wood today you will see a tree with several miniature crosses at the spot where the aircraft came down in remembrance of the pilot and navigator.

A few years ago, the Revd. Christopher Woods held a short memorial service to remember these two aviators who gave their lives so tragically through this accident. The service was attended by Herbert's only daughter, the Honourable

Davina D'arcy of Knayth, and two of his grand-children. It was a wonderful tribute to two very brave men. It was a very moving occasion for everyone who was present, especially when an R.A.F. bugler played the Last Post and Reveille.

New Vicarage

In the late 1930s a new vicarage was built overlooking the river Stour in Station Road between Ship Lane and Stour Lodge and was occupied by the Revd. Edward Harding. It was not used as a vicarage for many years and is now Emsworth House and privately owned.

Restoration Work at St Lawrence Church

In 1958 some major work was carried out to the chancel of St Lawrence Church. Some 30 years earlier in 1928 the Revd. Denis Bayley raised some floor boards under the choir stalls and discovered four ledger-stones (flat stones placed over a grave inside a church) of members of the Grimston family. These stones remained untouched for 30 years until the 5th Earl of Verulam carried out major work in the church. The Grimstons were the Earl's ancestors and he set about re-ordering and re-laying the chancel floor. All the Grimston ledger-stones were re-laid in an orderly fashion. Most of the stones remain in very good condition, as they had been hidden for generations and have not suffered centuries of foot-fall like those seen in most other churches. It was when this re-laying work took place that the foundations of an earlier building underneath the existing building were found, as mentioned earlier in this book.

Chapter 8

Bradfield today

Joined up Village

Over the years the village has lost its purely rural identity. Houses have been built on former agricultural land in all areas of Bradfield. Much of this was infill between existing buildings which resulted in the gradual joining up of Bradfield Street and Bradfield Heath to create one village nearly two miles long.

Examples of houses occupying former agricultural land are the four dwellings in Heath Road from Foxlease to Linderhof which were built in 1972 on land formerly belonging to Coppengers Farm. Foxlease was built on the site of a natural pond, and another pond lost at this time was on the corner of Wix Road, opposite the Village Maid public house. This site is now occupied by Orchard House built in 1964 and, as its name implies, the land was formerly an orchard. Other houses built on former orchards can be found in both Heath Road and The Street. Another example of a house built over a pond is Finials in Heath Road which was built in 1998 on the site of a modern ornamental pond in the grounds of the Ram and Hoggett pub.

A number of older dwellings have either been demolished and new buildings developed on the site or the existing building have been extensively redesigned. Examples of the former are Beer House Cottage in Station Road, Ivanhoe in Heath Road and Bo-Peep in Windmill Road. Old Hall House in Harwich Road, acquired its name not from an ancient house on the site but from the derelict wooden scout hut which formerly stood on the land. Greenacres in Station Road is on the site of Large's garage.

Sheltered accommodation for local residents was developed in the late 1980s - Dunning Close - and was opened in June 1988. The close was named in honour of Squadron Commander Edwin Dunning.

Royal Visit

Amongst the recent new housing in the village has been Rectory Gardens in The Street. The group of houses was built by the Rural Housing Trust as a response to the need for affordable homes for village people. The official opening of

Rectory Gardens by the Princess Royal, President of the Rural Housing Trust, took place on Wednesday 22 April 1998 and was reported in the June 1998 edition of the Bradfield Village Grapevine Magazine:

"What a glorious day it was for the visit of the President of the Rural Housing Trust, the Princess Royal, to officially open Rectory Gardens in Bradfield. The Princess was accompanied by her lady in Waiting and the Deputy Lord Lieutenant of Essex.

On her arrival Princess Anne received a warm welcome from the children of the Primary School, each waving a Union flag, and a group of village residents. Members of organizations involved in the scheme were presented to her. Her Royal Highness then unveiled a plaque to commemorate the occasion before accepting an invitation offered by Kim and Debra Smith to visit their home.

Princess Anne presented Paul Arthey with his Duke of Edinburgh Gold Award before being invited to join guests in the Community Hall, including some involved in a similar project in Great Bromley, for a light lunch. The lunch having been prepared by the ladies of the Women's Institute, as might be expected, was excellent and much appreciated.

On leaving the Princess warmly thanked the W.I. ladies who were presented to her."

HRH The Princess Royal with members of Bradfield's WI

During the period 1960 to the present day probably the most noticeable change in the village has been the gradual loss of the extensive orchards, once such a notable feature. At the time of writing no commercial orchards remain. The village has, however, retained a number of working farms including Bradfield Hall, Ragmarsh, Golden Ferry, Dairy House and a soft fruit farm in Wix Road.

As the village size has increased and villagers are now more independently mobile so the local amenities have changed. There is one combined village shop and post office at the far end of Heath Road. The garage and petrol station in the Street closed in the mid-1990s and the site is now occupied by two houses, one of which is named Forge Cottage reflecting the earlier use of the site.

Bradfield Celebrations – 1960 to 2000

Bradfield Village Association Community Centre

During the latter part of the last century Bradfield held an annual horticultural show and village fete. The event was held in the Bradfield Village Association (BVA) Community Centre and on the adjacent playing field.

The BVA hall was built in 1985 after extensive discussion and consultation with villagers over the previous few years. Ever since it has served the village excellently, providing great facilities for local clubs' regular activities (from playgroups to sports clubs such as badminton and football), as well as hosting other major village events.

At the Horticultural Show villagers competed in various classes for vegetables, flowers, arts and crafts and cookery for all age groups with certificates and cups awarded to the winners in each class. The show was followed by the fete where various games and competitive activities were enjoyed by villagers. These included a coconut shy, pony rides, dog racing and races for adults and children.

The event continued each year until the mid-1990s when it was discontinued. The Village Fete was restarted in 2010.

1977 saw the Silver Jubilee of Queen Elizabeth II. The village was decorated with bunting and celebratory activities took place on the playing field. As part of the celebration a competition was held for the best design for a village sign. This was won by Brian Winney. Running alongside this was a children's competition for the best illustrated map of the village.

The 50th anniversary of the end of the Second World War in Europe (V.E. Day) was once again an opportunity for the village to celebrate. One hundred people attended a V. E. Day tea held at the Bradfield Village Association Hall. Cakes were provided by members of the Women's Institute. An exhibition of wartime books and memorabilia was displayed and the entertainment included 1940s music played on a 1920s gramophone. Attendees also shared their memories of wartime. One lady recalled her part in making 3,000 pounds of jam with the W.I. during the war.

Bradfield's next celebration was for the Millennium in 2000. A Fun Day was held on Sunday 21 May 2000. The day proved to be very wet but, for all the people young and old who joined in the celebrations, it was a day to remember in spite of the rain.

There was an air of excitement in the village as people gathered in the streets to watch the decorated floats parade to the playing field. The parade was led by the Manningtree A.T.C. band. Floats were entered by the village churches, the Allotments Association, Bradfield Hall Farm, the Venture Scouts, Mistley Rugby Club, the Village Shop and East Coast Sounds. The parade also included an elderly red bus, tractors, a little girl on her pony, her brother in a spaceman's helmet on his tricycle, the Morris Dancers, the Maypole Dancers from the Primary School and a number of other fancy dress entries.

Judging of the entries in the parade took place on its arrival at the playing field, and prizes were presented. After this the new village sign was unveiled by its designer Brian Winney, who gave the following brief account of its origin and the significance of the design.

Top Left Section – part of the arms of the Grimston family who lived at Bradfield Hall in the 16th and 17th century and held numerous positions such as Master in Chancery, Members of Parliament, Recorders of the Harwich District, Master of the Rolls, and were created Baronets.

Bradfield Village Sign

Top Right Section – shows the three axes ("seaxes") which represent the county of Essex.

Lower Section – the five ears of corn represent the five arable farms within the village (as at 1977) - Bradfield Hall, Street Farm, Brocks & Brewses Farm, Stud Farm, and Nether Hall.

During the afternoon there was maypole dancing by the children from the village school, and Morris dancing by the Harwich Morris Men in the arena. The A.T.C. Band provided a musical interlude. Elsewhere in the field were sideshows including bowling for a pig, china smashing, bobbing for apples, a treasure hunt, a coconut shy, face painting and a raffle. A free Bradfield Millennium mug was given to each school age child.

In the hall were exhibitions of paintings, embroidery and other craft work and an interesting wall display of pictures of bygone Bradfield. Old scrap books were available to browse through.

At the end of the afternoon those who had braved the weather, gathered under their umbrellas, and led by the members of the brass section of the Ipswich Hospital Band, joined in "Songs of Praise". There was singing by the East Coast Sounds and the Revd. Andy Colebrooke gave a short address which was followed by the Lord's Prayer, the singing of Jerusalem and the National Anthem.

Extension to St Lawrence Church

A new extension to St Lawrence Church was completed in 2008. With the proceeds from the sale of the old scout hut in Harwich Road and additional support from The Friends of St Lawrence Church, the Parochial Church Council was able to fund the extension which provides a meeting room with kitchen and toilet facilities. This extension has enabled the PCC to hold meetings and events at the church that had not previously been possible.

The new church extension under construction in 2008

A new west door replaced the old one at the church in 2010. Made of oak the new door is engraved with two open books. As previously mentioned St

102

Lawrence was keeper of the church books and on the wall by the door is a plaque which relates the story of St Lawrence.

New west door

Bradfield Now

Bradfield today is a very different place to the Bradfield of yesterday. From a tightly knit, inter-dependent, agricultural community, the last century or so, with all the rapid changes in communications, travel and technology, has transformed the village into what it is today. Whilst some families have been here for generations many others are relative newcomers. Since 1881 the population of Bradfield has increased by about a third, but the number of houses has more than doubled.

There are, however, plenty of things still going on in Bradfield today, with numerous clubs and associations actively benefiting the community. There is still one shop (Bradfield Post Office & Store) at the Heath end of the village, two pubs (The Village Maid and The Strangers Home), two churches, a school and a village hall. There are also numerous, thriving, clubs and associations catering for the young and old, as well as everyone else in between.

The village hall and recreation grounds are managed, on a day to day basis, by The Bradfield Village Association, under the terms of a lease from Bradfield Parish Council. The Bradfield Village Hall Community Centre, to give it its full name, provides villagers with facilities for all sorts of activities. Apart from organising village wide events, such as the annual fete, the BVA is the home of Bradfield Rovers Football Club, Bluebells pre-school classes, the Over-60's Club, the bowls and badminton clubs.

Bradfield's Primary School is in Heath Road and is actively supported by Friends who organise a number of fundraising events each year. In recent years the school has been refurbished and has a large new hall and computer suite.

In addition to church activities the St Lawrence Church Room and the Methodist Hall are also used regularly as meeting venues by several clubs and associations. The St Lawrence Room is regularly used by the church Guild for their meetings and monthly tea-parties, the Buggy Club and the Friends of St Lawrence Church for its various fundraising events. The Methodist Hall hosts the Men's Breakfasts, the Ladies' Breakfasts, WI meetings, the Baby & Toddler Group and the Scout Troop.

Other clubs include the Footpath Walking Society and the Allotment Association.

The excellent bi-monthly "Grapevine" magazine, which is delivered free to every household in Bradfield, keeps villagers informed and up-to-date on what is going on in the area and has regular contributions from many of the village's clubs and associations.

The Future

The main objective in writing this short history of Bradfield has been to give readers a brief insight into what has happened in the village over the centuries. It is hoped that this book is just the beginning and will form the basis for further historical studies. At each stage along the way the authors have had to resist the temptation to investigate further certain lines of enquiry. To do so would have significantly delayed its publication, but there are many unanswered questions that need further research.

A large amount of historical material has been amassed during the writing of this book. It is hoped that some readers will be interested in developing and maintaining a historical archive about Bradfield, which will at some future date be freely available to anyone interested in Bradfield's past.

Index